THE TWENTY TRECENAS OF THE TZOLK'IN

A White Shaman's Guide to Using the 260-Day Tzolk'in Clock

Written and Experienced by The White Shaman

EAST 26TH
PUBLISHING

The Twenty Trecenas of the Tzolk'in

Library of Congress Cataloging-in-Publication data is available
ISBN: 978-1-7348856-6-8

Editing, book layout and cover by Krista Huber

10 9 8 7 6 5 4 3 2 1
First printing edition 2020

East 26th Publishing
Houston, TX

www.east26thpublishing.com

Good things take time. Great things happen all at once.

This book teaches you how to make things happen all at once using the power of our creator.

TABLE OF CONTENTS

THE TWENTY TRECENAS OF THE TZOLK'IN

THE WHITE SHAMAN OF CANYON DE CHELLY

After thirty years of working as an engineer, raising a family, and living a "traditional" American adult life, Venus transited behind the Sun on June 8, 2004. This created a significant shift in my energy and started my interest in the Maya culture—particularly, their concept of time and how it functions. The Tzolk'in became a significant point of interest and the subject of my studies. In my opinion, the way the Tzolk'in works resonates with humans better than the Gregorian calendar. The western Gregorian Calendar, marked by 365 days (366 every 4 years), tracks the solar (or, seasonal) year. Although I lived by this sense of time, I innately understood there was a different energy for each day, but those energies did not correlate with anything I knew or understood.

Contrastingly, the Tzolk'in Calendar (though I regularly refer to it as a "Clock") marks 260 days, each with a unique energy. The passing of the 260 days is considered a "Tzolk'in Round." The most significant historical representation of the Tzolk'in Clock is the comparison of the Madrid (left) and Aztec Fejervary (right) codices shown here. This perfectly connects the two illustrations.

Between 2004 and 2010 I read every book I could find on the subject of the Tzolk'in, Maya time, and the Maya culture/civilization.

In 2010, I met with Carlos Cedillo and Dr. Carl Johan Calleman, experts on the interpretation of the Traditional Maya Calendar, to study Maya time keeping. I then spent the next seven years traveling across the world visiting Maya ruins and attending Maya ceremonies in order to immerse myself in the spiritual world and further my studies in the Tzolk'in.

In 2013, I was made a Maya Shaman during my travels to study Maya ruins in Guatemala. It is was around that time that I began to understand myself as the "White Shaman," as I was told to bring my learnings to Texas.

Perhaps the name came to me because soon afterwards, I found the White Shaman (shown here) and the doorway in 2017 during my visit to Canyon de Chelly in the Navajo nation of the United States, during which I lived 40 days and nights in a Navajo hoogan exploring the four corners of the Navajo nation.

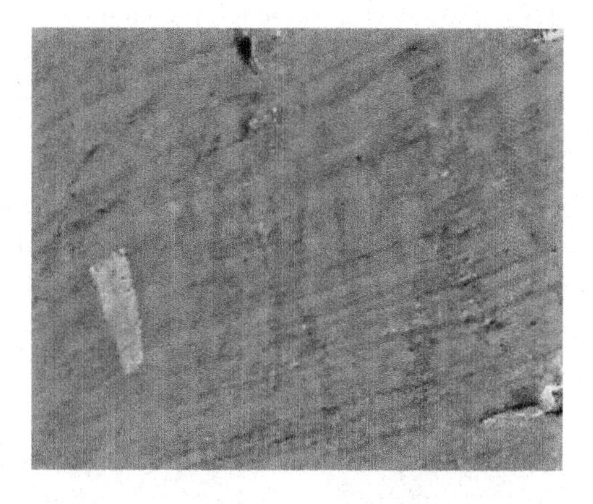

All of these events, and my experience being welcomed by my Dine' hosts, enlightened my understanding of how the Tzolk'in mentally relates to the four directions. This way of seeing the Tzolk'in explains our personal mind and our inter-personal relationships, especially with friends, workmates, family members and marriages, in the four directions and why the four directions are so important in the Maya culture.

During my studies, I developed several theories about the influence of the Tzolk'in Clock and its relationship to us as individuals and as a collective conscious. I also came to understand several similarities between the Navajo and Maya cultures and have developed a theory in which the Navajo hoogan can be used as a three dimensional representation of the Tzolk'in Clock.

Here is a list of my experience and studies:

1977 – Given the book Three Magic Words by US Anderson by my grandmother and did the 30-day mental diet as suggested

1984 – Developed the 3D image of my mind

1985 – Graduated college

2004 – Venus transited behind the sun

2004 to 2008 – Student of Maya language, history, culture, and especially the Tzolk'in (as depicted in the Madrid codex)

2009 – Wrote my first manuscript about my understandings of Maya time

2010 – Met Carlos Cedillo and Dr. Carl Johan Calleman in Wimberly, Texas to discuss Maya day-keeping

2011 – Attended a thirteen-grandmother ceremony in New Braunfels, Texas and experienced a profound spiritual awakening

2012 – Attended a ceremony in Llano, Texas to watch the second Venus transit in front of the sun. This is when I began my travels

2012 – Attended the Lothlorien Peace festival in France. Met Maya Guatemalan grandmother Elisabeth Aurojo, Maya Colombian Paco Quiroga, Dr. Masaru Emoto from Japan, Dr. Carl Johan Calleman, and Grandmother Carola Esparza from Chili.

2013 – Visited Maya ruins in Belize and Guatemala. During the middle of this trip I was made a Maya shaman in Tikal and told to bring my understanding to Texas. This is when I began to write as "White Shaman." This trip included visits to Cahal Pech, Xunantunich, Naranjo, Tikal, Uaxactun, Flores, Lamanai, Cuelo, and the Belize zoo

Early 2016 – Visited Olmec, Aztec and Maya ruins in Mexico at Piedras Negras, Teotihuacán, Huautla, La Venta, Agua Azul, San Cristobal de las Casas, Tonina and El Tajin

Late 2016 – Spent two nights inside of Canyon de Chelly and had a strong urge to return to the canyon

2017 – Spent 40 days living in a hoogan in Chinle, Arizona and explored the four corners of the Navajo nation. Blanca Peak = East, Mt. Taylor = South, San Francisco Peaks = West and Mt. Hesperus = North.

2018 – Published 20 articles on www.mayanmajix.com for each of the twenty trecenas: Crocodile, Jaguar, Deer, Star, Light, Transformer, Storm, Road, Serpent, Flint, Monkey, Seed, Earth, Dog, Night, Wisdom, Offering, Wind, Eagle and Star.

INTRODUCTION

This book is a summary of my studies while living on the Tzolk'in 260-day-round method of experiencing time which is completely different than living on the Gregorian (European) calendar. If you are ready to experience life in harmony with natural time, this book will present topics such as:

- How to manifest your reality,
- Why you get along with some people and have difficulty communicating with others,
- How the Tzolk'in calendar is connected to your mind and body,
- What it means to become an elder,
- What happens while you sleep and how to identify with your sleep consciousness,
- And, potentially, how to find the right person for your life.

This book explains the Tzolk'in calendar like no other book. It delves into a deeper, spiritual understanding of the Tzolk'in as we look at its multi-dimensional aspects, its diagrams, its message and its connection to our mind, body, and spirit. It contains powerful insights to connect with your living spirit. The Maya had a word for this life spirit called *Ak'bal* or *your house*, a human construct. Within your house there is a flame of life. Knowing how time interacts with your human experience will enlighten your understanding of inter-person relations and personal manifestations. I call this "living on Tzolk'in time." This book is a guide to using the Tzolk'in as a time piece. It helps to see how all 260 days work together for both you and all life around you.

The Tzolk'in first appeared in recorded history around 500BC in the Olmec culture of Mesoamerica. In 1549AD, apparently, all books of the Maya people were destroyed and only four know manuscripts survived: the Dresden, Madrid, Paris, and Grolier. It is from the Madrid codex that we see the Tzolk'in calendar depicted and most of this book's information is derived from this picture. I am hopeful more pre-Columbian books will be discovered in Mesoamerica and made available for us to discover more truths about the Maya understanding of time in the classical age.

There is another illustration of the Tzolk'in calendar in the Aztec Fejervary codex. By comparing the Aztec and Maya versions I have found many aspects of its meaning. The first aspect is that both depictions are meant to be viewed in three dimensions, but could only be displayed on paper in two dimensions. Most of this book is based on seeing the Tzolk'in in three dimensions. I think this is a revolutionary way of living with time.

There are many sources of information on which I gain my basic understanding of the Tzolk'in and how it relates to daily life. Mazatzin Aztekayolokalli explains how the Tzolk'in is embedded in the Aztec sun calendar in this video (https://www.youtube.com/watch?v=0b9vqrjK2lQ). His website is http://azteknology.com.

Jill Taylor's book A Stroke of Insight explains how the left and right brain are connected to our mind. Ian Lungold explains the works of Dr. Carl Calleman and the nine levels of consciousness. Using these references combined with the Madrid and Fejervary codice Tzolk'in, and many other references, we are able to see the true meaning and power of the living on the Tzolk'in as a timekeeper that tells you when to plant your seeds and how to grow them into manifestations of your reality.

If you are prepared to open your mind to new ways of thinking about each day's energy and how to best interact with each day, then I welcome you to keep reading. This book contains many spiritual relations to your mind, your consciousness, your asleep self and our connections to a life-giving greater spirit.

Much of this book contains information that I have learned by practicing shamanism with thousands of people. All of this practice is based on the popular belief that 13-Ahau was October 28, 2011 as would 4-Ahau align with December 21, 2012—two well-known dates on the Gregorian calendar.

This book will discuss the twenty 13-day weeks of the Tzolk'in calendar for a total of 260 days. This is not to be confused with the eighteen 20-day months of the Ha'ab calendar. The Ha'ab 365.25 solar calendar is a separate, but related calendar of the Olmec, Aztec and Maya. The Ha'ab will be briefly discussed and a connection shown between the two calendars.

I do not see the Tzolk'in as a calendar, but as a clock or timing device. My several reasons for this that will be discussed in detail. As an analogy, imagine that the hour hand on the Tzolk'in Clock goes from trecena to trecena and the second hand goes from day to day.

This book is not purely scientific, as it will take too much time to prove many of the concepts offered about every person's experience. However, once you have read it, you can decide if it has improved your way of living with time. My work is not complete, but to a point that it is meaningful.

There are many parts to this puzzle to be solved. You should, however, be familiar with the evolution of consciousness as presented by Dr. Carl Calleman and Ian Lungold. These concepts are not discussed in academia, but they are appreciated by contemporary Maya. My short-coming in the composition of the theories presented in this book is that I have not actually lived with the Maya and my ideas come from practicing Shamanism locally in Texas where few know about the Tzolk'in way of keeping time.

Just as the Maya Tzolk'in is a unique measurement of time, the Maya method for writing is also unique. In short, their writing uses a picture and two vowels to make a word. You can make a billion words with 360 pictures and 9 vowels. Since so many pictures were used over the years and in different areas of Mesoamerica, it is difficult to compare pictures as the same or unique, and hence know the total. All other forms of written language either use just pictures or phonetic symbols.

Different Maya people celebrate the beginning of the Tzolk'in on different days. This book explains the meaning of both 1-Crocodile and 8-Monkey as the beginning. In short, 1-Crocodile is the day it starts for you and 8-Monkey is the day it starts for all of us.

This book goes into detail about our human mind and our consciousness. Most people do not know why we need to sleep, nor what happens when we sleep. This book will discuss the difference between our awake selves, our asleep selves and how our consciousness transfers between the two selves. It will discuss the interactions of our left brain, right brain, and mind, both personally and collectively. Since everyone was born on one of the 260 days, we are all connected to it. The Tzolk'in Clock is a spiritual way to live with time as an individual and as a group. The Maya people who use the Tzolk'in (Chol Q'ij) believe you are born with the energy of the day and resonate with that day's energy ("Secrets of the Mayan Calendar Unveiled" presented by Ian Xel Lungold on September 6, 2003 Okanagan University College in Vernon, Canada). Knowing your Maya birthday helps you know yourself and your personal outlook in relation to everyone else.

This book also lets you view the Tzolk'in in three dimensions. Using the Navajo hoogan, due to its many similarities, we can see how the Tzolk'in gives us meaning with the four directions, our chakras, and internal flame.

Here is a summary of the unique outlooks offered in this book:

- Faces of the Tzolk'in Clock versus corners of the Tzolk'in Clock
- How your seven chakras connect with the Tzolk'in Clock
- The four directions east, north, west, and south and your personal connection to them
- We will envision the Tzolk'in Clock in 3D and use the Navajo hoogan as a tool for comparison
- How the furnace of a Navajo hoogan compares to your internal flame
- The meaning of your *Nawal*, or, *sleep self* and why it is important to know
- How to best use the power of a thirteen-day trecena to manifest your reality
- How to best use the power of a 260-day Tzolk'in round to manifest your reality
- What is the difference between starting the Tzolk'in Clock at 7-Dog / 8-Monkey versus 13-Ahau / 1-Crocodile
- Does the Tzolk'in Clock spin at the top of the tun calendar or does it spin the tun calendar?
- Learn about your awake self (or, enslaved self) versus your asleep self
- How do we connect to the Tzolk'in Clock? What benefits do we give to it?
- See the connection between the solar (Ha'ab) calendar and the Tzolk'in
- Is there a soulmate connection where you can easily share your conscious?
- Is there an ebb and flow to each day's energy and when does the energy change from one day to the next?
- Learn to plant your seeds or packaged goals and how to mature those seeds into fruition using the Tzolk'in Clock
- See how the Tzolk'in Clock is a map of the human mind based on left and right brain, awake and asleep self, thoughts, choices and morals

I believe that the Tzolk'in, as represented by the Maya and Aztec, is meant to be viewed in 3D with you sitting in the center. The 260-day timer starts on 1-Crocodile on the east face and ends on 13-sun on the southeast corner. Every 65 days, it changes direction from east, to north, to west and then to south. Each direction consists of three 13-day trecenas (or, 39 days) on the face wall and two 13-day (or, 26 days) trecenas on the corner wall. This book goes into much detail and uses the Navajo hoogan as a tool to better envision it as I believe it should be viewed.

Statistically, forty percent of us are born on a corner wall of the Tzolk'in Clock and sixty percent of us are born on a face wall. This book will discuss the difference between the four faces: east, north, west, and south; and the four corners: northeast, northwest, southwest and southeast. Based on my research, there is a face and corner connection. For example, people born on the east face and the northeast corner are "teammates". There are four teams on the Tzolk'in: team east, north, west, and south. Which team are you on? On which team are your friends, classmates, and family? My research shows that you naturally get along with people born on your team. Also, you help them to facilitate their intentions. My research leads me to believe that people born on a face are like team coaches and people born on a corner are like team players. Collectively, each team works together during the 65 days that the Tzolk'in is on their direction. Someone born on the same day as you with the same outlook feels like a brother or sister to you.

Another, and perhaps the most fascinating aspect of viewing the Tzolk'in Clock in three dimensions, is that each of the 260 days look inwards so that every outlook has another outlook that directly faces it! This is what I call the "soulmate" connection between two people. With the soulmate connection it easy to share your consciousness with another person who is directly facing yours. Healthy relationships can be one of the most satisfying experiences. This book will help you know how you relate to your significant others. Statistically, the chance to meet a soulmate connection is 1 in 260.

Each of us have a different one of the 260 outlooks. My birth outlook is 9-Star in Maya and 9-Rabbit in Aztec and my elder outlook is 4-Wisdom in Maya and 4-Vulture in Aztec. 9-Star/Rabbit is a day known for its fertility. The rabbit is commonly shown as a scribe in pre-Columbian Maya art. As an elder, I have two outlooks, which gives me more perspective on life than before I turned 52. People do not get older, they become elders. This book discusses what it means to be an elder.

The book is not definitive. It is simply an inquiry into native Maya. Volume II will include the Maya's feedback on my ideas. These codices have resurfaced after hundreds of years of European dilution of the original intentions. The purpose of this book is to broadcast and collect ideas to be later published. You should have a good understanding of the Tzolk'in to appreciate this work.

It was on the Dog trecena, 2018, that my first article was written about the next Akbal trecena. Therefore the 20 articles section of this book starts with the Akbal trecena. These articles have been updated since they were last published and will continue to be updated each Tzolk'in round. Interwoven in all 20 articles are the following topics:

- •Face vs. corner
- •Chakra connection
- •Team east, north, west and south
- •3D view / hoogan compare
- •Akbal meaning (hoogan comparison)
- •Nawal meaning (sleep self)
- •From seed to fruition – 13 days
- •From seed to fruition – 260 days
- •8-Monkey vs. 13-Ahau (Light)
- •Fixed in place vs. spinning
- •Enslaved vs. Un-enslaved (asleep)
- •Aging of Cha'ak
- •Ha'ab embedded into the Tzolk'in
- •Soul mate theory
- •Daily Tzolk'in in hours
- •Offering / receiving on east / west face
- •The Tzolk'in Mind (left brain / right brain)

Some may say this type of content is "New Age" and they would be correct. The spirit of my writing would be lost in academia. I have a passion for the Tzolk'in. These articles are a presentation of my ideas in hopes we meet and discuss them. It is a sharing of what I know so you can teach me what you know. Together, we can learn and educate each other, because there is so much of the Maya culture that has been lost.

Thank you to Ian Lundgold, Birgitte Rasine and Michael Shore for giving me a voice. A special thanks to my deer stormy spirit who inspired me to write these articles and Carlos Cedillo who taught me what he learned from Don Alejandro and consistently opened the path to many experiences for me.

TOPICS ON THE TZOLK'IN CLOCK

THE NAVAJO HOOGAN & THE TZOLK'IN CLOCK

This picture was taken on my first trip to Canyon de Chelly on 13-Water (July 22, 2016). The following February/March of 2017, I spent forty days and nights in the Navajo nation, traveling the four corners and living in this hoogan. I spent my time in the local canyons and mountains and took excursions to the four corners of the Navajo nation, with Navajo guides, in search of evidence of Tzolk'in and other Maya-to-Navajo similarities. As we discussed Dine' calendars, it was interesting to see how Navajo people enjoyed the idea of a 260-day spiritual calendar. One of the best evidence I found of this is the construction of their hoogan. The Tzolk'in image in both the Madrid and Fejervary codices are two-dimensional depictions of a three-dimensional timekeeper. Folded upright, you view each side on a wall, like the inside of a Navajo hoogan, as it also has eight sides (four walls and four corners). The east side of the Tzolk'in would be placed around the front door of the Navajo hoogan, which faces east.

Imagine yourself sitting in the center of the hoogan (where the cast iron stove normally sits) watching the sun rise, facing east, before the rays of the sun touch your body. You are surrounded by eight walls and a roof. The floor is dirt with a few spiritual holes between you and the west wall behind you. The shadows from the doorway move along the wall each day as the sun travels its seasonal cycle. This is a good way to live on the Tzolk'in Clock and spiritually connect with time. The articles in this book will go further in-depth about the connection of the Tzolk'in Clock to the Navajo hoogan.

No Navajo person remembered having a "calendar" before their European indoctrination into the Gregorian calendar. All we can do is speculate with a few clues. There are courts in the Navajo nation that resemble Maya ball courts. Both the Navajo and Maya have twin heroes in their creation story (Popol Vuh). Maya chocolate in Maya decorated vases have been found in New Mexico at Chaco Canyon. But did the Navajo people have the imagination or Maya education to make their sacred home in the shape of the Tzolk'in Clock? The Navajo hoogan is shaped identical to the Tzolk'in Clock, which has the same 3 trecena side, 2 trecena corner pattern! Logistically, it is 1500 miles from Mexico City (northern Maya civilization) to Arizona (Dine' civilization). Walking just 20 miles a day, it would take 75 days to make this journey. For comparison, it is 1000 miles from Mexico City (northern Maya civilization) to San Salvador (southern Maya civilization)—the full extent of Maya civilization. It is practical to believe the two cultures could have, at one point, shared a common ancestry or belief structure.

There is also evidence of North American Indian plate art that show similar patterns to the Tzolk'in.

THE TRECENAS ON THE TZOLK'IN CLOCK

Viewing your life through your native Tzolk'in outlook is a life changing experience. Knowing where you are located on the Tzolk'in gives you a profound spiritual connection to our creator.

This location is where your spirit connects with a greater life force. After using the Tzolk'in Clock for a few 260-day rounds, you learn how to interact with each day's energy. You learn how to use time to manifest your self-created reality. Knowing that a greater life force gives you tremendous strength and confidence.

Each of us have a unique (1-in-260) outlook and, therefore, our individual perspective and point of view is different. My experience with a day's energy is different than yours, as we are seeing it from a different outlook (unless we are born on the same Tzolk'in birthday). Our perspectives vary from the same to slightly different to perpendicularly different to completely opposite.

I chose the terminology "clock" (instead of the more common "calendar") for this book. You can make a comparison as the trecena is the like the hour hand and each day is like the minute hand. The Tzolk'in is often called a calendar, yet it is not tied to any astrological objects like the lunar, solar or Venus calendars. As you experience the Tzolk'in you will come to understand why it is so difficult to call it a calendar.

A trecena is 13 days of time (in comparison to a "week" on the Gregorian calendar). There is a total of 20 trecenas on a full 260-day Tzolk'in round. Each trecena has an underlying energy and a destination energy. For instance, the trecena of 1-Crocodile carries the crocodile energy underneath the trecena as the energy heads to the last day, 13-Road. It is like walking up a 13-step staircase. The fundamental energy of the trecena is held between the first and last step.

A trecena can also be viewed as a seven-level pyramid. On the crocodile trecena, the first step is 1-Crocodile energy. The seventh step and top of the pyramid is 7-Deer. Then you walk back down the 7-level pyramid to the bottom step, which is 13-Road. Many people have heard the expression "hump day" referring to Wednesday as the middle of the work week. This expression can be applied to the seventh day of a trecena. The seventh day of a trecena is the highest point and it is downhill from there.

Ian Lungold uses another metaphor for a trecena—that of a seven gear truck. The first day of the trecena is first gear. The second day of the trecena is neutral. The third day of a trecena is third gear and the fourth day is neutral. This pattern repeats until the last day—the seventh gear. To continues his metaphor, when the truck has enough momentum from seventh gear of the previous trecena, you can jump start to begin the first gear of the next trecena. You can use this pattern of energy in your daily life.

Another metaphor is that of a river. The first day is like dew on the leaves. The third day is like trickles of water to a stream. The fifth day is like a stream. The seventh day is like a river, and so on. The second, fourth, sixth, eighth, tenth and twelfth days are like that of calm and placid water.

Most people measure time on the 365-day Gregorian calendar and a 24-hour clock. People use this to set up meetings, make appointments and schedule deliveries. The Gregorian calendar has holidays on which families get together and weekends during which people collectively take time off. Few people realize the controlling power this has on our collective consciousness. The Gregorian calendar is based on the location of the sun in the sky from summer to winter and back again. It is a materialistic calendar and may explain our current situation on earth, as people use only the Gregorian calendar of time. In contrast, the Tzolk'in Clock is a spiritual way to measure time.

There are humanistic relationships to the patterns of 13 and 20 within the Tzolk'in. The Tzolk'in consists of 20 trecenas and your body has 20 digits (fingers and toes). A trecena is a 13-day week. Your body has 13 major joints: the neck, shoulders, elbows, wrists, hips, knees and ankles. 20 times 13 is 260 days. There is a 260-day gestation cycle of a human.

This book attempts to explain personal, spiritual and sacred components of the Tzolk'in as ways to interact with time and bring focus to living each day with a mindful purpose and action.

A trecena has an ebb and flow to it as each day interacts with the next and previous day. You can learn to use the seven active days and six resting days of the trecena to your highest advantage. For example, if you have a project that takes 13 days to complete, you could gradually begin your project on the first day of a trecena. Then you can take a rest from it on the second day. One the third day, you put more work into it and then rest on the fourth day. On the seventh day on the trecena, or "hump day," you should applying maximum effort. By that day, most of the hard work is completed, but you still have the rest of the trecena to complete the project. So later in the trecena, even though you are doing more to complete the project, the effort does not appear to be as difficult. By the thirteenth day (the end of the trecena) you should have finished, and it is a day to relax and get ready for the next trecena's project.

I also believe that a day's energy begins at sunset of the previous day. The energy then lasts all day and ends the sunrise of the following day. During the night, the previous day and the next day's energy overlap. During the daytime an energy does not overlap with the previous or next day's energy. So, a Tzolk'in day's energy lasts about 36 hours. Dividing 36 by 13 gives roughly 2.8 hours of time for each of the 13 inflections of a day's energy. This 2.8-hour sections ebb and flow like a trecena. The maximum flow of each day's energy lasts for 1.4 hours before the sun is highest in the sky and then for another 1.4 hours. Each day's energy flows like this: Sunset (±1.4 hours) is the first wave. Midnight is the third wave. Sunrise is the fifth wave. Noon is the seventh wave. Sunset is the ninth wave. Midnight is the eleventh wave. And, finally, the next sunrise is the thirteenth wave of the previous day's energy and the fifth wave of the next day's energy.

My experiences have led me to believe that people born between sunset and sunrise may take on either of the day's energy. Here is how the change from day to day occurs: As the sun sets, the energy of the next day will emerge. At midnight, the levels of energy cross. As the sun rises, only the energy of that day will be present. As the sun sets, the energy of the next day gradually emerges. Both energies are shared during the night. People born at night will feel which energy is right for them—which energy was in their first breath.

Also, the twenty consecutive day intentions flow together as you experience them. The crocodile is an energy of emergence, followed by the wind energy of thought, followed by the house energy of spirit, followed by the seed energy of personal intentions, followed by the serpent energy of life, followed by the transformer energy of afterlife, followed by the deer energy of stability, followed by the star energy of fertility, followed by the water energy of gratitude, followed by the dog energy of playfulness, followed by the monkey energy of choices, followed by the road energy of destiny, followed by the reed energy of heaven, followed by the jaguar energy of nature, followed by the eagle energy of sight, followed by the wisdom energy of understanding, followed by the earth energy of power, followed by the flint energy of cutting, followed by the rain energy of cleansing, and , finally, followed by the sun energy of new growth. Then the cycle repeats 13 times for 260 days. When you know this, you will start to feel how days flow together, like the jaguar changing to the eagle who changes to the vulture as it returns to mother earth, sometimes with the power of an earthquake. Once you are at one with the Tzolk'in Clock, your spiritual awareness of a day's energy intensifies, and your feelings resonate with our creator and our collective consciousness. The difference is the Gregorian calendar is like living in black and white and the Tzolk'in Clock is like living in color.

There are many sources that describe each day's inflection and intention. I typically use the website www.mayanmajix.com. They have a daily Tzolk'in subsection on their website. It also has a calculator on which you can enter the Gregorian date and find the corresponding Tzolk'in day. The best way to know a day's intention is to know what the day is and experience it yourself. After a few Tzolk'in rounds you will begin to learn it yourself. Their calculator is aligned with October 28, 2011 being 13-Ahau on the Tzolk'in. All websites of Tzolk'in, Chol Q'ij and tonalpohualli match this correlation. Only European archeologist and astronomers have mismatched days. There is also a popular Dream Spell interpretation developed by Jose Arquelles that has no association to this book.

I believe the Tzolk'in Clock drives all the celestial bodies like the solar cycle (Ha'ab, Gregorian, Julian), the 360-day tun cycle, the lunar cycle and the 584-day cycle of the Venus. The Tzolk'in Clock also aligns, internally, with your spirit. Every day you wake up to one of the 260-days and each of these days is associated with one of 13 inflections and one of 20 intentions. It connects us to everything else.

The Tzolk'in Clock also connects to your mind and consciousness. For instance, the north face of the Tzolk'in Clock starts with the transformer intention. This is the corner stone of the north direction. The north face of the Tzolk'in Clock consists of the Transformer (Death) trecena, the Rain

(Rainstorm) trecena and the Road (Grass) trecena. The northwest corner consists of the Serpent (Snake) trecena and the Flint trecena. The transformer energy is carried throughout the north face and the northwest corner. The north face is the veil between our enslaved conscious self and our freed collective conscious self. Every night when you fall asleep, your consciousness passes through the north face veil of the Tzolk'in Clock. Knowing where your consciousness goes every time you sleep, answers the same question as to where we came from before being born and where we go after death. The Tzolk'in Clock shows the answer. The pattern for manifestation is, at first there is the creation of an idea. Then there is a spiritual realization of the idea. Then there is a collective agreement to create that idea. Then it is put back on you to physically make it happen.

THE FOUR DIRECTIONS OF THE TZOLK'IN CLOCK

There is an association with the four directions. The energy of the Tzolk'in Clock shines on one direction at a time. Each direction consists of five trecenas, three on the face and two on the corner. For instance, the transition from the south to the east is like this: The energy of the east face begins on 1-Crocodile, after the past five trecenas ended, on 13-Light. The entire south side of the Tzolk'in Clock goes dark. Its intention has been fulfilled. On 1-Crocodile the entire east face and northeast corner of the Tzolk'in Clock lights up. The energy builds from 1-Crocodile, to 2-Wind, to 3-Night, to 4-Seed, etc. This energy builds up through the trecena. On 1-Crocodile, all people born on 1-Crocodile pour their intentions into our collective consciousness. And the next day it builds to 2-Wind. And builds and builds until 13-Reed. That day begins a higher trecena. It starts on 1-Jaguar and builds until 13-Transformer. That day begins on 1-Deer, the third trecena on the east face of the Tzolk'in Clock. After that trecena begins 1-Light. 1-Light is the first day on the northeast corner. People born on corners not only pour their intentions into our collective consciousness on their birthday, but also that of all the people born on the face. The faces collect the intentions of the east like droplets of water and the corners spray the intentions that started with 3-face trecenas into the collective consciousness, like seeds from a flower. This process repeats for all four directions. The two 7 days (7-Transformer and 7-Storm on the northeast corner) are especially free to spray their intentions of the entire 3-tracena face and 2-tracena corner into the collective consciousness. And then after 13-Serpent, the entire east side of the Tzolk'in goes dark. It is time for the north face and northwest corner to do their work, starting on 1-Transformer.

Folding the 2D Tzolk'in calendar as depicted in the Madrid and Fejervary codices into 3D, clearly shows four walls and four corners with you in the center, just like a hoogan. Each wall of the Tzolk'in has three trecenas, one going up the right side of the wall, one going across from right to left, and one going down the left side of the wall. Each corner has two trecenas, shown with curves, not angles, in both codices. These curves give a flowing effect to each corner, like a propeller. Together a wall and a corner make up a team and there are four teams on the Tzolk'in: Team east, Team north, Team west and Team south.

Have you ever been standing next to a stranger and felt comfortable talking to them? It is likely that both of you are on the same "team." People born on the same "team" make good friends. The Tzolk'in Clock explains the reason for feeling comfortable with people on the same "team." Furthermore, people born on the same trecena will feel like brothers and sisters in their friendships—especially if they are born on the same day!

There are differences between people born on the face of the Tzolk'in Clock and people born on the corner. The way the trecena pattern works is that face people rely on the corner people to have their intentions offered to the collective consciousness. Statistically, 60 percent are born on a face and 40 percent are born on a corner. Personalities of face and corner people are different, as corner people tend to stir things up and face people tend to like more stability. When the direction of your Tzolk'in birthday lights up, it is your time to participate with our collective consciousness and you (and all members of your team) carry this burden of time for five trecenas, or, 65 days.

MAPPING YOUR FAMILY AND YOUR LOCATION ON THE TZOLK'IN CLOCK

Imagine living with the Maya around 800AD in the late classic period. I imagine people born on the day's intention would be part of the day's ceremonies. If today was 1-Crocodile, then all the people born on 1-Crocodile would gather at the temple. They would be available for others to ask questions or just discuss the day's energy with them. Elders (discussed below), who received 1-Crocodile as their new outlook, would also be included. People born with the first and thirteenth inflections would stay at the temple the entire trecena and be involved with special ceremonies. The best way to get to know a day's intention is to be with people born on that day. If you had a curiosity about a day's intention, you could visit the temple that day and meet with people born on that day.

Your Tzolk'in birthday is the day to let the world know your intentions. It is your day "to make a wish," just like is customary on the Gregorian calendar. However, on the Tzolk'in, the world will listen! People naturally want to be with you on your day. You can learn about the day's energy when being around people on their day. That is why there is a natural reason to have a birthday party! Maya birthdays are days of intense resonance with the day's energy. Maya trecenas are similar, but on a slower vibration. You have a slight "breeze to your back" on your trecena. If, for example, you were born on a 1-Flint, 2-Flint, 3-Flint, etc. then the Flint trecena will have a pleasant vibration with your natural energy. If you became an elder on a Flint day, this trecena will give you an uplifting vibration.

Elder Outlook

After living 52 Ha'ab years and 73 Tzolk'in rounds, you have experienced every day-to-day combination between the Ha'ab and Tzolk'in. Don Alejandro, a spiritual leader of the Maya, teaches that your elder outlook or, elder intention, is eight days after your birthday outlook. So if you were born with the 1-Crocodile intention, then you will have the 9-Monkey elder outlook. This new outlook is the same as what is commonly referred to as your "mid-life crisis." However, it is not a crisis; it is enlightenment. You have seen the past 52 Ha'ab years through one outlook. When you turn 52 years old, you get a new outlook, and your vision of life is improved from mono-optic to bioptic. Elders have perspective on things due to having two viewpoints at once. They see things through two outlooks rather than just one.

Tzolk'in Birthdays

Also, birthdays have a spiritual meaning, so making a birthday wish really connects with our collective energy. Since the day's energy resonates with your energy on the Tzolk'in Clock, your wish flows into our collective energy. It is also a reason that people naturally want to gather around you and celebrate the day's energy on your birthday. Being around people on their Tzolk'in birthday brings you closer to the day's energy.

Tracking a newborn's birthday is easy on the Tzolk'in Clock. You also look forward to their Tzolk'in birthdays to celebrate their energy. It is also easy to track and congratulate them on 300 days, 400 days, etc. Then it's 520 days (their 2nd Tzolk'in birthday) and you continue to remember to congratulate them for turning 600 days, etc. The sense of Gregorian years becomes less important and every day becomes a kind of birthday celebration. It is also fun when people ask your child's or grandchild's age and you give it to them in days. Watch as they try to convert it!

Mapping

Consider each dot shown on the Tzolk'in as a different outlook. It is rare that two people born on the same Tzolk'in day get to interact. This helps to explain how people are always seeing the same things differently. Chances are that everyone in a situation has a different outlook. It should be noted that our collective consciousness sees all 260 outlooks at once and the Tzolk'in Clock is a map of our collective interactions.

Knowing everyone's Tzolk'in birthday helps our social interactions. Collectively we become aware of our strengths and weaknesses. Knowing more than one person born on the same day is helpful to see their similarities. You have 260 unique interactions with all others. And all others have their unique 260 interactions. Therefore, your interaction with a person born on 6-Star, for example, will be a unique (1 in 260) interaction. Anyone born on a different day than you will get a different perspective of the same person born on 6-Star. It is helpful to map out where you and your friends and family are on the Tzolk'in Clock. The Deer trecena article has a sheet that lists all 260 Tzolk'in days as they flow from east, north, west and south. You can print this and use it to mark your friends and family. It helps to remember or share their Tzolk'in birthdays. Each row on this list is a team. Team East, Team North, Team West, and Team East.

Looking at the Madrid and Fejervary codices of the Tzolk'in, each dot is a unique outlook on life. The Tzolk'in, viewed in 3D, is a way to see from where each person gets their unique point of view. This way of viewing your interactions with other people lets you know their outlook for seeing things. Learning about these interactions, collectively, enhances communication and builds trust in a community living within a spiritual way of understanding time. The structured life, living with the Gregorian calendar, is almost completely at odds with the Tzolk'in Clock. People living on the Gregorian calendar become more machine-like and less human, without realizing it. It is like they cannot put their finger on what is wrong and, instead, try to stay distracted with their materialistic obligations. Use the Tzolk'in calendar as a journal for a year or two and you will easily see the difference. Writing thoughts on March 3 or September 27, for instance, do not give any useful spiritual meaning to your day. Comparatively, entering thoughts on a 7-Serpent or 3-Crocodile day, for instance, will resonate your thoughts with the day's natural energy.

By mapping people who are in your circle of friends, you can see how they interact with you and with each other. Here is an example: Taking the people born (circled in white in the picture on page 16), you can better understand their interactions. It starts to make sense when people on the same team get along better. When two people face towards each other (imagine this image in 3D with the walls and corners folded upright) they can almost read each other's minds. People born on the same trecena feel like brothers and sisters. As well as there is a coach / player relationship with people born on the face and corner of the same direction.

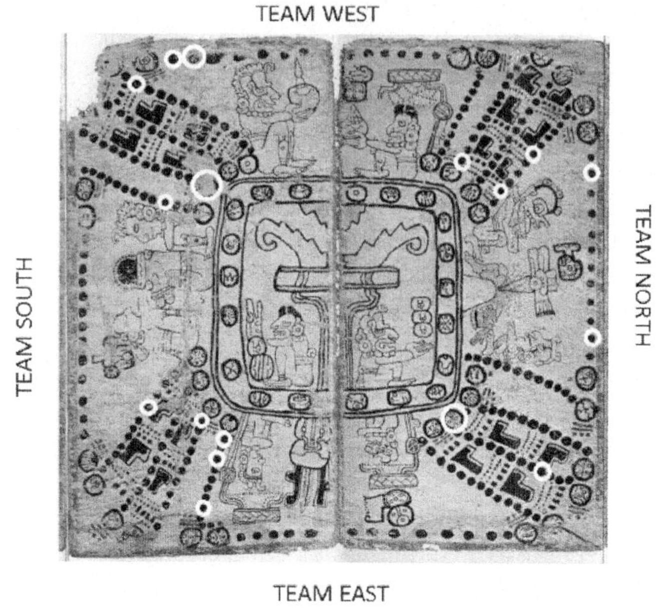

TEAM WEST

TEAM SOUTH

TEAM NORTH

TEAM EAST

SOULMATES

Does the Tzolk'in Clock hold a special connection?

It is interesting how two people born on exactly opposite days interact. By opposite, it means, when folded into a 3D view, each of the 260 dots points directly at one of the other dots. How would these two people interact? Could this be a "soulmate" interaction? I believe these unique 260 relations have telepathic communication. There is soulful communication at every level of thought, body, and heartfelt experience. When couples have soulful communication, their experience is majestic. You can see it in their presence together.

Sitting inside the Tzolk'in Clock, facing east and with the walls folded upwards, you can see there are outlooks that directly face each other. For example, 12-Ahau/Sun, on the south face, is directly opposite of 1-Storm, on the north face. 1-Water, on the south face, is directly opposite of 12-Dog on the north face. People born on the thirteenth day of a trecena have special relationships with each other. For a long time, I was not sure if the first day on the trecena interacted with the twelfth day or the thirteenth day. The uniqueness of people born on the thirteenth day, along with recent research, has led me to believe that the soulmate relationship is between 1 and 12, 2 and 11, 3 and 10, etc.

A soulmate relationship is also about balance. The weight of time on the Tzolk'in Clock separates each outlook by one direction. The soulmate relation is always north to south or east to west. I often see boyfriends and girlfriends connected with partners who are on the same team. Since the feeling of friendship exists, it is easy to confuse a friendship relation with soulmate relation.

It would be good to have a retreat with people representing one of the 260 days on the Tzolk'in Clock. We could prove this soulmate relation and research other relations. For instance, would four people from each side of the Tzolk'in Clock, collectively, have a better view on an issue than four people from the same side of the Tzolk'in Clock? Perhaps, individually, we lack the capstone of our consciousness and collectively we can gain complete understanding. We all have God-like power within us, but it has been capped off. Imagine collectively unlocking the full power of the Tzolk'in Clock.

PLANTING SEEDS

The Tzolk'in Clock is a tool to plant seeds and have them yield fruit. Each 260-day round, we plant seeds (wishes, affirmations, intentions, etc.) in our mind, heart and spirit. However, it is helpful to know when and what brings them to life. The Tzolk'in Clock shows you. Each phase of growth is naturally tracked according to Tzolk'in Clock. The planting starts on the east face, then northeast corner, then north face, then northwest corner, then west face, then southwest corner, then south face and ends on the southeast corner.

East Face

Planting of the seeds begins on 1-Crocodile, the first day on the east face of the Tzolk'in Clock. Your seeds were prepared 20 and 40 days before 1-Crocodile. Your seeds are offered on the east face of the Tzolk'in Clock.

Northeast Corner

After three trecenas on the east face of intention, your seeds are actively released to your sleep consciousness, the north face.

North Face

Our seeds, planted on the east face of the Tzolk'in Clock, go through the rainstorm trecena deep within our sleep consciousness. Then seeds must travel the Road trecena to be presented to our collective consciousness for judgment. Prepare your new self for the west face of the Tzolk'in Clock.

Northwest Corner

After three trecenas (39 days) during which your sleep consciousness has worked on your seeds, they are actively released to our collective consciousness.

West Face

The west face consists of the Monkey, Seed and Earth trecenas. The Seed trecena travels across the top of the west face with 8-Monkey along the way. The Seed trecena is deeply connected with our collective consciousness. It is the time our future selves are judged for creation and the time that we update our collective consciousness. The west face, and especially the Seed trecena, interacts with our collective consciousness, our morals, our knowing right from wrong and making choices. You are gaining a new perspective on your future self. It now seems possible to have everything you requested on the east face of the Tzolk'in Clock. Ideas for how to make it happen and physical action towards that wish are flowing.

Southwest Corner

Your seeds, planted on the crocodile trecena, must interact with the physical realm to come to fruition. It is during the southwest corner that our seeds come to fruition. The seeds of your future self were presented, examined, and contemplated by our collective consciousness on the west face of the Tzolk'in Clock. Living in a hoogan when the Tzolk'in Clock is on the west face, you can feel your future self being examined. Your seeds are now ready to enter your physical reality to emerge as fruit on the south face of the Tzolk'in Clock.

South Face

When viewed in 3D, the south face of the Tzolk'in is to your right, and the Water trecena flows along the top of the right wall. During the south face and southeast corner, our seeds will become reality. The south face of the Tzolk'in Clock starts with the Wisdom trecena. The south face is when the interaction between the Tzolk'in and Ha'ab, or Gregorian calendar, mostly occurs.

Southeast Corner

The south face is the time to reap your harvest from the seeds planted on the east face. The southeast corner is the time to package your new seeds for the next Tzolk'in round and a time and enjoy the fruits of your labor. The full effect of the southeast corner makes 13-Flower a natural day of celebration and it flows well with the day's natural energy.

HOW TO USE THE TZOLK'IN TO MANIFEST

Life gives us seeds and seeds have the power of our creator to manifest into food for humans. The Tzolk'in Clock works the same and the cycle repeats every 260 days. You will learn to sync your goals (or seeds) with this natural cycle. You will learn when to expect the universe to deliver your manifestations. You will gain confidence knowing that our creator will deliver to you all that you desire and that our collective consciousness will allow on a set schedule.

The manifestation aspect of the Tzolk'in Clock starts on the east, then moves counterclockwise to the north, then west, then south. The start of the Clock, 1-Crocodile, is the day to start planting your mental seeds, or goals, to bare fruition. Each trecena along the way is a place to tweak your 260-day goals and to set new 13-day goals. Use the ebb and flow of the 13 days to bring your thoughts into reality. Looking at the Tzolk'in as a Clock puts each day into perspective with the whole.

This process is depicted in the Madrid codex version of the Tzolk'in. A man on the west is asking for something. The man on the east is receiving something. The man on the south is tied up in his body, and the man on the north is released from his body. In the center is a tree with flames. This is the Akbal—the furnace/spirit inside of yourself. Days on the Tzolk'in have spiritual energy (not offered on the Gregorian calendar). It is interesting how many New Year's resolutions fail. This is because you are doing it all by yourself on the Gregorian calendar. Contrasted, planting seeds on the east face is a way that your spiritual self can assist you, using the 260 days of the Tzolk'in. Tend to your seeds during each of the 20 trecenas, so it comes to fruition. Not all seeds planted come to fruition on the first Tzolk'in round. Like plants, they may take more than one Tzolk'in round to bear fruit. It is important to take care of the whole garden in your mind. This may be your first time to use the Tzolk'in Clock. It is like saying a prayer, but with the idea that the prayer is a seed to nurture on each of the 20 trecenas of the 260-day Tzolk'in Clock.

The Tzolk'in Clock gives you a timeline to manifest your reality. Many people make wishes or resolutions and expect quick results. Sometimes, they give up on their dreams. The Tzolk'in 260-day round keeps you involved in the process of manifestation. First you offer your seeds, then you sleep on them, then our collective consciousness gets updated and incorporates your manifestations, then they are presented to you in this physical realm. This is a 260-day method to connect with our collective consciousness and manifest your requests. Relax with confidence, knowing your spiritual self has your intentions and will be actively working using every day's energy on the Tzolk'in Clock.

The east face (Crocodile) of the Tzolk'in Clock is about thought.

The north face (Transformer) is about our right brain.

The west face (Monkey) is about the collective morals.

The south face (Wisdom) is about our left brain.

The Tzolk'in Clock is a way to transform our lives from "chasing the dollar" on the Gregorian calendar to, instead, using your spiritual self to deliver your reality. When using the Tzolk'in Clock, you already have your reality presented to you. Chasing materialistic wealth takes a lot of external energy. Spiritual wealth is done with thoughts surrounded by calm, placid water. Be mindful of how, when and where you choose to put your energy.

The Gregorian calendar way of living gives you self-created life. The Tzolk'in Clock way of living gives you our creator's power. The Tzolk'in Clock is the timekeeper while your spiritual self takes care of the plants growing in your heart, soul, and mind. Keep the materialistic way of living to a minimum so it does not interfere with your natural way of creating. For hundreds, if not thousands of years, the Olmec, Aztec, and Maya lived on this spiritual calendar.

The Gregorian calendar captures your time and deflects your spiritual sense of time. Waking up in the morning on the Gregorian calendar, do you ask yourself, "What day is it?", "What time is it?", and "How much free time do I have before getting ready?" In contrast, waking up on the Tzolk'in calendar, you ask yourself, "What is today's energy?", "How am I feeling in relation to what I know about the day's energy?" and "What's the best way to handle today?" There are no 9AM meetings scheduled for the Tzolk'in Clock. Save that energy for the time to take physical action to fulfill your destiny.

The Tzolk'in 260 calendar depicted in Codex Fejérváry-Mayer shows the pattern of the seed to flower:

Starting on 1-Crocodile (the east direction), we plant our seeds.

Starting on 1-Transformer (the north direction), we meditate and use our asleep self and dream state to manifest and grow our seeds into plants.

Starting on 1-Monkey (the west direction), we mediate with our collective conscious on manifesting our plants into reality.

Starting on 1-Wisdom (the south direction), we actively make our dreams come true in the real world.

There are eight walls in a hoogan and eight on the Tzolk'in Clock.

The east direction consists of the east face and the northeast corner.

The north direction consists of the north face and the northwest corner.

The west direction consists of the west face and the southwest corner.

The south direction consists of the south face and the southeast corner.

Here is what happens on each wall:

East Face

Happy New Year! Create and plant your seeds by giving awareness to the fertile ground. This trecena is about shaping the landscape of your mind, heart, and spirit. We are planting new seeds and moving around plants on the east face.

Northeast Corner

It is during these two trecenas that our seeds are being collected by our collective consciousness—the place we go when we are asleep. These trecenas transition us from the east face of the Tzolk'in Clock to the north face. The north face of the Tzolk'in Clock begins with 1-Transformer. The transformer face is the veil between awake and asleep. It is the portal that our consciousness passes each time we sleep and again when we wake up. These two corner trecenas transition our seeds and prepare them for the north face.

North Face

Our seeds are being "grown" in our collective consciousness during the north face. This is the time that your spiritual self (which I often refer to as your Nawal) helps to create your physical self's reality. You are not alone in this realm; we are collectively working together. Each time you fall asleep, your consciousness leaves your mind. It is in that realm that our collective consciousness interacts. It is like all the physical cells of your body go to different places and then re-unite the moment we wake up.

When the Tzolk'in Clock is in the north face, it is a time in which trust and faith come into play. Do you trust your spiritual self? You must trust that obstacles presented in your physical realm are there to help you find your new reality. Using the Tzolk'in Clock and trusting your spiritual self to bring your physical self reality is the key to creating your reality.

The north face of the Tzolk'in Clock is the time to envision your future self, life, and surroundings. The seeds you planted on the east face are being farmed out by your sleep consciousness. Physically, there is not much that can be done. The growth happens naturally. Your best effort now is positive meditation and peace in your heart. Good things take a lot of work. Great things happen all at once. The north face is about letting those great things manifest in our spiritual selves so they can be created in our physical reality.

Northwest Corner

Your seeds have grown during the north face. The northwest corner is about polishing the final details before being presented to the west face for judgement, where all our seeds are sorted out to create everyone's future reality. This is an organic process.

West Face

The west face is about morals, choosing right or wrong, and is always changing with our collective consciousness. As we pass through the west face our seeds will update our collective morals. It is a two-way process, in which we collectively decide who gets what and we all get our new morals for the next Tzolk'in round. The start of your seed process is the east face. The start of the updated morals is on 8-Monkey, the center of the west face.

Southwest Corner

The fruits, or, manifestation process starts on the south face when you physically make your moves to accept the fruit. The southwest corner is a time to prepare your physical connections as well as your internal flame for the south face of the Tzolk'in Clock.

South Face

The Maya version has a man enslaved in his body and mind. This represents our consciousness when we are awake and enslaved in our body. The mental relation of the Tzolk'in Clock has the Water trecena crossing the left side of our brain. The left side of our brain controls language, logic, mathematics, reasoning, and our five senses. The Tzolk'in Clock is telling us that it is time to use these facilities. This is the time to harvest the seeds we planted on the east face of the Tzolk'in Clock. It is also the time to start thinking about the new seeds we will plant for the next Tzolk'in round.

Southeast Corner

This is the time to reap the abundance your fruit. The seeds we planted on the east face began bearing fruit on the south face. The southeast corner is the end of the harvest. It is a time of gratitude and sharing, a time of personal abundance and gracious acceptance. A time to give thanks to our creator, spiritual self, and personal self for our choices made this past Tzolk'in round.

The Tzolk'in is a tool that enables your ability to manifest your reality. Plant your wishes on the east face like planting a seed in your mental garden. Plant as many seeds as you want in your net when it is time to harvest. Plant them with loving packages in the fertile soil of the east. With these seeds, you have the power of our creator, our spiritual selves, and the ebb and flow of 20 trecenas to manifest your reality.

THE TZOLK'IN'S CONNECTION TO THE HA'AB AND TUN

Unlike any other calendar, the Tzolk'in and Tun do not follow the path of a celestial object like a solar year nor lunar month. Their only interaction is with day and night and 260-day and 360-day cycles. No one knows for sure why they came into our consciousness and from where they were derived. However, dates are commonly written based on both the tun and Tzolk'in in classical Maya art. It is the Ha'ab calendar that follows the 365.25-day solar year. I have made a few observations about the Tzolk'in's connection with other calendars like the Ha'ab and the Tun.

The Temple dedicated to the plumed serpent, or *Kukulcan* in Chichen Itza, shows nine levels of the tun calendar and connects with the Ha'ab in two ways. First, there are 91 steps on each side for a total of 364 steps. Second, and more famously, each spring and fall equinox, the shadow from the northwest corner makes a trecena pattern that rises from the head of the serpent at the base to the top of the pyramid as the tail. There are 7 patterns of sunlight and 6 patterns of shadow. The fastest cycle of the nine-level tun calendar is the 260-day Tzolk'in, which would be appropriate at the very top of the Temple of the Plumed Serpent. I have not found diagrams, nor photos, of the top level of Chichen Itza prior to its reconstruction that matches a 20-day cycle (Uinal on the Tun calendar). That is not to say that it never existed on top. I can not image a better place for a hoogan shaped structure.

Statistically this happens on the 1-Serpent once every 180 Ha'ab years. The 1-Serpent day would begin on the bottom and rise to the platform which would be 13-Earth. The serpent energy is underneath the seven arcs of sunlight and the six arcs of shadow. Does something special happen when the serpent trecena begins on an equinox? Is that another measure of time? Looking forward from year 2020, the next possible time would be the vernal equinox on March 20, 2024 but it might also miss by a day or two.

The connection of the Tzolk'in to the Ha'ab calendar is embedded inside the four corners of the Tzolk'in as depicted in the Madrid codex. The 360 days of the tun, the 18 months of the Ha'ab, and the 5.25-days of the Wajeb are shown.

I believe that the Tzolk'in Clock is the generating force for all other calendars. I can envision the Tzolk'in as a fan or propeller of time. We know it explains the difference a day makes and that feeling of *Oh, today must be my day!* The only question that remains is if the Tzolk'in fixed or spinning. In other words, does time pass through the Tzolk'in to create change or does the Tzolk'in spin through time to create change? Either way, it would be difficult to prove this concept.

1-CROCODILE VS. 8-MONKEY

There are two different views on when the Tzolk'in round begins. Some say 1-Crocodile on the beginning of the east face and others say 8-Monkey at the middle of the west face. I say it starts at both places, but for different reasons. It starts on 1-Crocodile for personal reasons. 8-Monkey is the day of our new collective consciousness.

Traditionally, the Tzolk'in Clock starts on 1-Crocodile, which begins the east face in the hoogan analogy. Have you ever heard of New Year's resolutions on the Gregorian calendar and their reputation for failing? Unfortunately, the Gregorian calendar does not have a spiritual connection and is misleading in this regard. However, the Tzolk'in Clock begins with making resolutions, or, rather, begins with planting seeds of intention for the upcoming Tzolk'in round. Your seeds are then carried around all 260 days, with 13-Flower serving as a type of New Year's Eve. It is a time of celebration and gratitude for fruits of your seeds planted. The following day (1-Crocodile) is the first day to direct new intentions into the collective consciousness. Your new intentions are directed towards the collective consciousness during all three east-face trecenas of the Tzolk'in Clock. There is joy felt, as you know your "New Year's resolutions" are being heard at the right time.

Your faith in this process will improve each time you experience a new Tzolk'in round. This is an organic process like the gestation of a human, which also lasts about 260 days. The seeds you plant on 1-Crocodile are like the moment an X and Y chromosome connects to form a new human. That's when the Tzolk'in Clock begins its magical life force on each one of your planted seeds.

Others celebrate 8-Monkey as the beginning of the Tzolk'in round. 8-Monkey is the day our collective consciousness gets updated. It is the reason for the incremental changes in collective morals. Today's issues are different than our parents' and grandparents' issues. Our collective consciousness is continuously updated, and 8-Monkey is the day to celebrate it.

8-Monkey happens as our consciousness passes the midline of the Tzolk'in Clock. This day is shown on the Tzolk'in Fejervary and Madrid codices crossing from right to left at the mid-plane. This same imagery is found in relation to our corpus callosum, going from the right brain into the left brain. Time changes from passive to active. As our collective consciousness is updated every 260 days, it is difficult to relate to the mindset of the ancient people. Language and location may have been barriers, but humans all had the same collective consciousness. The collective consciousness is continually being updated and thoughts today will seem outdated in the future. It is also the reason many people begin thinking the same ideas and thoughts each round.

CHAKRAS

The Tzolk'in calendar connects your mind, body, and spirit to time. The Tzolk'in is a personal and humanistic way of keeping time. It is multi-dimensional and carries our collective consciousness through time. Looking at the human depicted in the center of the Aztec version of the Tzolk'in Clock, shows energy of the second, third, fifth and sixth chakras. Each of these energies connects to one of the corners of the Tzolk'in Clock. The feet, heart and head connect to the first, fourth and seventh chakras, respectively.

Various parts of the Tzolk'in Clock connect to a human (representing you) in the center of the Aztec version of the Tzolk'in. The Crocodile trecena is on the crown chakra energy. This is just one of many humanistic qualities of the Tzolk'in Clock. Thoughts are received through our crown chakra and processed through our heart chakra using the balance of our feet (grounding) chakra. As the Tzolk'in Clock progresses your seeds of thought into reality, it must pass through the humanistic chakra energies. This gives life to our Tzolk'in round, as it connects our awake self with our spiritual self and our creator.

The day you were born has an assigned chakra that is more prevalent than the others. It's easy to spend too much energy focused on your birth chakra and that will lead to unbalance. I once asked a family of Mazatec shamans how to make my heart chakra larger and they said my heart chakra is fine, but my birth chakra is too large. Learn which chakra energy points at your Tzolk'in birthday and use it to benefit yourself and others. The goal is to balance all seven of your chakras and knowing this helps.

THE TWENTY TRECENAS

The following chapters are a composition of twenty articles written and published in real time by The White Shaman as he lived a full Tzolk'in round with the intention of learning the unique energy of each day in the twenty trecenas of the Tzolk'in Clock.

AKBAL

This image of the Tzolk'in is presented as a 260-day clock. The trecena of House (Akbal) starts in the top left corner and is underlined. The background image is from the Madrid codex, penned around 1562 AD. The Tzolk'in calendar encourages and places focus on living each day with a mindful purpose and action. Take a minute to look at this before reading further.

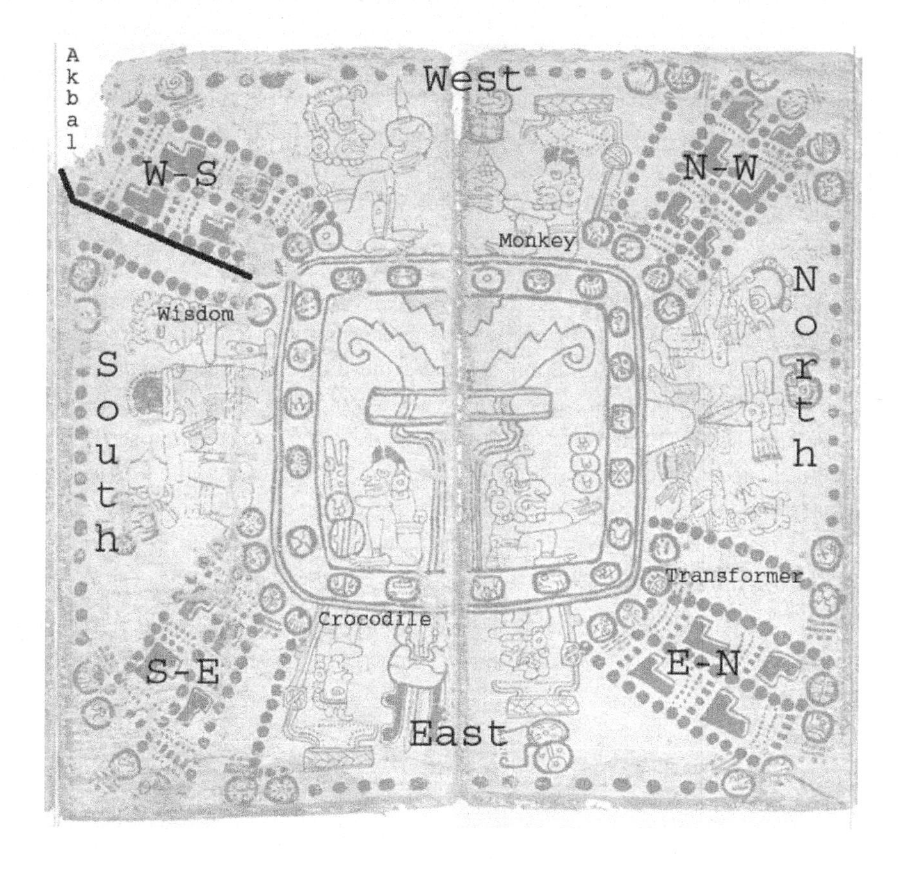

It's important to see how each day relates on the Tzolk'in Clock, just like hands relates to a 12-hour clock. The Tzolk'in Clock starts on the east (Crocodile) then moves counterclockwise to the north (Transformer), then west (Monkey), then south (Wisdom) for a full 260-day rotation, also called a Tzolk'in Round. Each direction (east, north, west and south) is written in the ancient Maya text, near my English translation. Do you see them?

How the Clock Works

The start of the clock (at 1-Crocodile) is the day to plant mental seeds, or goals that could bare fruition 260 days later—similar to New Year's resolutions. Each new trecena along the way is a place to tweak your Tzolk'in round goals and to set new 13 day goals. Learn to use the ebb and flow of the 13 days to bring your thoughts into reality. Looking at the Tzolk'in as a clock puts each day into perspective with the whole. Look at how it's presented to us. For instance, a man on the west is asking for something. The man on the east is receiving something. The man on the south is tied up in his body, and the man on the north is released from his body. Our consciousness is released from our bodies every night and is enslaved in our body every day. In the center of the Tzolk'in Clock is a tree with flames. This is the Akbal—your furnace; the spirit inside of yourself.

Today we start the trecena of 1-House (Akbal).

The Tzolk'in Clock should be viewed in three dimensions, yet it is drawn in two dimensions. As part of my white shaman training, I spent 40 freezing cold days in the Navajo nation, traveling the four corners and living in a hoogan. The hoogan is very similar in structure to a three-dimensional Tzolk'in Clock. During my stay in the Navajo nation, we spent most of our time chopping wood for the families' furnaces. In the hoogan, the furnace is placed in the center, just as the tree of fire is placed in the center of the Tzolk'in Clock. Do you see the image? That is the furnace to your house (Akbal) on the Tzolk'in Clock.

When you wake from sleep and open the hoogan door, with the furnace keeping you warm, and see the vision of dawn, this is the energy of House (Akbal).

1-House (Akbal)	What fuels your internal furnace/spirit?
2-Seed	Let your inner seed emerge. Plant seeds in your mind that fuel your house/spirit so they can start to manifest.
3-Serpent	Feel your internal furnace (Akbal) ebb and flow. Put your energy in a direction that nurtures the seeds to fuel your spirit.
4-Transformer	Remember your relations with others.
5-Deer	Remember your dreams and survey the landscape.
6-Star	Think ahead to the next trecena with bold intentions to shine.
7-Water	Tend to your duties (physically and spiritually). Go with the glow and continue to nurture your seeds.
8-Dog	Enjoy yourself. Appreciate your internal furnace.
9-Monkey	Be playful with friends. This is a day for new opportunities.
10-Destiny	Feel it coming. Appreciate that your seeds are growing. Go with the flow and seize the opportunities presented to you.
11-Reed	Talk with your creator. Pray.
12-Jaguar	Work together ethically.
13-Eagle	Get out and visit with a friend. Keep the bigger perspective.

WISDOM

Today, 1-Wisdom starts the first trecena on the south face of the Tzolk'in Clock. Looking at the image from the Madrid codex, the next three trecenas go around an enslaved man. You can see his arms and legs bound and his head encapsulated. Directly opposite on the Tzolk'in, is the north face. Three trecenas, starting with 1-Transformer, go around a man set free from his body. It's interesting that a flint blade is used to cut the man.

This Tzolk'in image is a two-dimensional depiction of a three-dimensional clock. The previous article discussed how it could be mapped on the inside of an eight-sided Navajo hoogan. Viewed from the center of the hoogan, while facing east, the south face would be to your right and the north face would be to your left. The south and the north faces are directly pointing at each other, when viewed in three dimensions.

Starting today, these next three trecenas involve the use of our intelligence (speaking, counting, logic, music and dance) and our connections with the physical world using our senses (touch, taste, sound, sight and smell).

Every day you wake up to a new energy. Using the 260-day Tzolk'in Clock to create your reality has a pattern. At first there is the creation of an idea. Then there is a spiritual realization of the idea. Then there is a collective agreement to create that idea. Then it's put back on you to physically make it happen. It's during these next trecenas that we physically make it happen, using our minds and bodies.

1-Cib (Vulture/ Owl)	After 13-Eagle, today we take the wisdom learned from the west and apply it to the south. What can we do to manifest our reality?
2-Caban (Earth)	With the wisdom gained yesterday, plunge deep into yourself to find the tools you need for tomorrow.
3-Etznab (Flint)	Use the tools from yesterday to weed your mental garden, to remove guilt, and to guide new ideas that you want to see in reality.
4-Cauac (Storm)	Let the powerful 4-Storm blow away yesterday's work and cleanse your spirit, heart and mind.
5-Ahau (Sun)	Let light shine into the freshly trimmed areas to give new growth. Feel the light in your hand. Do something with your power.
6-Imix (Crocodile)	Dive deep into your spirit to bring out ideas and desires—especially the ones you initiated on 1-Crocodile.
7-Ik (Wind)	Let your connection with our creator empower your vision.
8-Akbal (Night)	Bring your intentions into your house. Remember your work from the past trecena. Let it fuel your furnace.
9-Kan (Lizard)	Start your manifestations for the next Tzolk'in round by transforming ideas and desires into seeds that can be given on the east side of the Tzolk'in Clock. Fully imagine your reality. Decorate your seeds.
10-Chicchan (Serpent)	Let the birthing energy of the seeds grow. Let the waves of newness flow.
11-Cimi (Death)	Daydream today. Dream your reality. Imagine living in it today. Feel it as though it's real.
12-Manik (Deer)	Get real today. It doesn't all happen mentally. Use your physical body and intelligent mind. Calmly make your reality happen.
13-Lamat (Rabbit)	Give thanks to your creator. Look to the moon.

WATER

The Tzolk'in calendar connects all humans using time, mind, body, and spirit. It's also meant to be viewed in more than just two dimensions. As a three-dimensional representation of the Tzolk'in, consider you are in the center of an eight-wall room (like a hoogan) and you are facing east out the door, towards the sunrise. When viewed in 3D, the south face of the Tzolk'in is to your right, and the Water trecena flows along the top of the right wall. This is the trecena to actively make your seeds fruit in your reality. During these next few trecenas, it is a time to reap the fruit from the seeds we planted on the crocodile trecena.

Here, the Tzolk'in 260 calendar is depicted in Codex Fejérváry-Mayer.

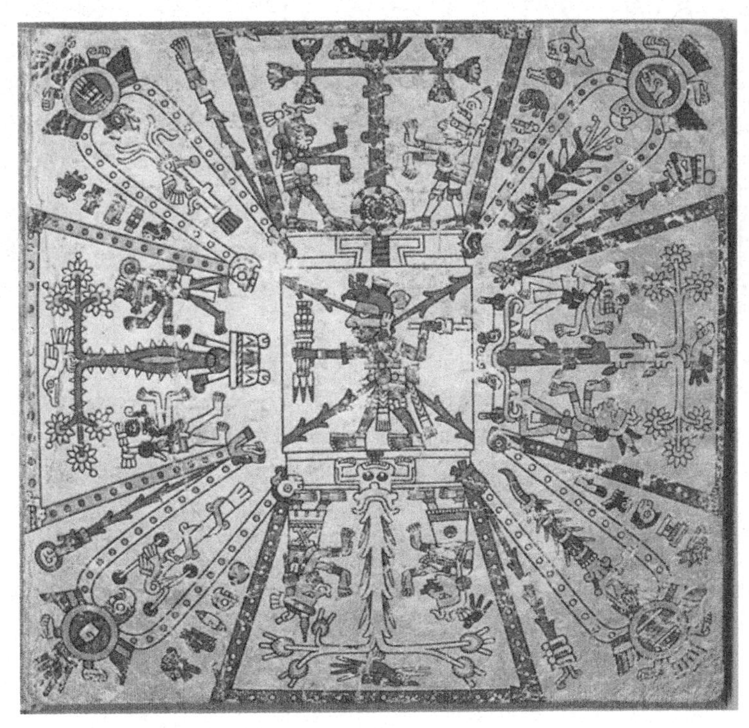

The pattern of seed to flower to fruit is shown within the Aztec version of the Tzolk'in Clock. This is very well described here: http://www.mexicolore.co.uk/aztecs/ask-us/sacred-birds-flowers-and-day-lords.

Starting on 1-Crocodile (the east face of the Tzolk'in Clock), we plant our seeds.

Starting on 1-Transformer (the north face), we meditate and use our asleep self and dream state to manifest and grow our seeds into plants.

Starting on 1-Monkey (the west face), we mediate with our collective conscious to manifest our plants into reality.

Starting on 1-Wisdom (the south face), we actively make our dreams come true in the real world.

The four phases of seeds to fruit shown on the Aztec Tzolk'in here:

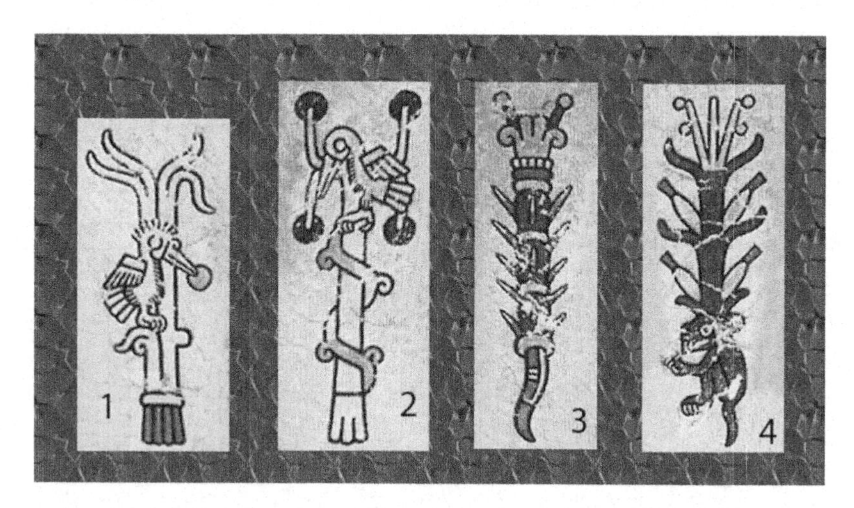

The mental relation of the Tzolk'in Clock has the Water trecena crossing the left side of our brain. The left side of our brain controls language, logic, mathematics, reasoning, and our five senses. The Tzolk'in Clock is telling us that it is time to use these facilities. This is the time to harvest the seeds we planted on the east face of the Tzolk'in Clock. It is also the time to start thinking about the new seeds we will plant.

The Water trecena is the one in which to take action. The whole trecena is about going with the flow. Or, like William Shakespeare quote:

There is a tide in the affairs of men, which taken at the flood, leads on to fortune. Omitted, all the voyage of their life is bound in shallows and in miseries. On such a full sea are we now afloat.

We can compare the water trecena on both the Aztec and Maya versions of the Codex Fejérváry-Mayer and Codex Madrid Tzolk'in calendars. The Aztec version has a Cacao tree with a parrot representing the south. The southeast corner has a tree bearing fruit. The Maya version has a man enslaved in his body and mind. This represents our consciousness when we are awake and enslaved in our body.

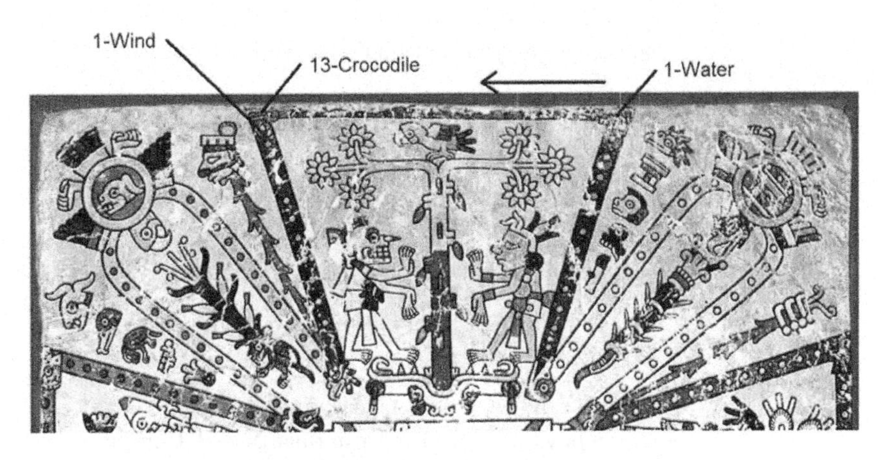

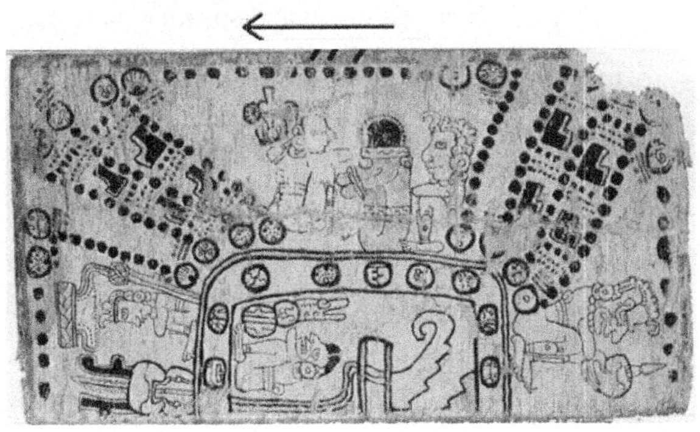

1-Water	This trecena starts with dew on grass and builds to streams in the forest and unto ragging rivers by the end of the trecena. So hold on to something and enjoy the ride!
2-Dog	There is an animal called a water dog in Belize. It's an animal that lives in the water and behaves like a dog. This is today's energy.
3-Monkey	Meditate, in peaceful surrounding, with a magnified focus on love—loving thoughts, loving words, loving intentions and loving actions.
4-Road	Let your destiny arrive. The flow of water is more powerful than you, so let it do the work for you.
5-Reed	Give thanks to our creator and everything brought to us from our creator.
6-Jaguar	Give thanks to nature and earth.
7-Eagle	The highest day of the Tzolk'in round. You can see clearly everything on all days of the Tzolk'in on this day.
8-Wisdom	This is going to be a very mental day, and it can be wearisome. It's a day to process yesterday's information.
9-Earth	Dreams can feel so real. Jaguar Wisdom explains how we have a physical Nawal and a spiritual Nawal. Connect with your physical Nawal and spiritual Nawal.
10-Flint	Today's energy is about staying awake to the moment. There is a lot of work to do on you today. Use the mirror to cut out negativity from thoughts and feelings.
11-Storm	The energy of Storm will build throughout today, and many of those larger clippings might flow away into nothingness and leave room for new loving intentions.
12-Light	Surround yourself with mother nature and rejoice with loving thoughts, loving intentions and loving actions.
13-Crocodile	We have 40 more days left in this Tzolk'in round. Today, start thinking about what seeds you will plant on 1-Crocodile, the beginning of the new Tzolk'in round.

WIND

As described in the past few articles, imagine yourself sitting inside of an eight-sided Navajo hoogan. You are in the middle, facing east towards the door. West is behind you, south (shown below) is to your right and north is to your left. The Tzolk'in Clock is meant to be viewed in three dimensions.

The Tzolk'in Clock has eight sides, like a hoogan, with four faces (east, north, west and south) and four corners (east to north, north to west, west to south, and south to east). The Wind trecena is the last trecena on the south face (right side) of the hoogan (shown outlined in yellow). After the wind trecena are the two trecenas on the southeast corner. I call the combination of the three south-face trecenas and the two southeast-corner trecenas, "team south." The Wind trecena begins the last three trecenas of the Tzolk'in Clock. During these next three trecenas we gather the fruits from our seeds and set the intentions for our new seeds to be planted on the Crocodile trecena—the beginning of the east face and the first day for "team east."

Let's consider the Wind trecena's relationships on team south. Have you ever been standing next to a stranger, and just felt comfortable talking to him or her? It's likely that both of you are on the same "team." People born on the same team make good friends. The Tzolk'in Clock explains the reason for feeling comfortable with people on the same "team." Looking again at the figure above, the first day of the south face is 1-Wisdom (bottom right of picture). This is the day that the weight of our collective consciousness is released from "team west" and placed on shoulders of "team south." Everyone on "team south" has their Tzolk'in birthday on one of these five trecenas. People born on 1-Wisdom begin the process, then 2-Earth, then 3-Flint, etc. until, after all 65 days, the weight of our collective consciousness is place on "team east" beginning on 1-Crocodile. Each team shares the burden of time for 65 days. All other teams are resting until it is their turn.

My research has led me to believe that people born on the same team naturally get along with each other, more so than people born on different teams. Furthermore, people born on the same trecena will feel like brothers and sisters in their friendship—especially if they are born on the same day!

Fascinating Facts that Connect us to the Tzolk'in Clock

- The interlinking of the Tzolk'in and Ha'ab (the 365.25 day calendar) gives life changes at 13, 26, and 52 years. At 13 years old, it is typically a day to celebrate a boy's manhood. Later, as an adult, it's good to wait until you are 26 to make any major life changes that will affect your next 26 years. You become an elder at 52 and are given a new outlook. And, there is a celebrated charm when turning 104, which should be everyone's personal goal.

- There are around 260 days is the gestation cycle of a human. From the time of conception until birth is around 260 days. You experience a full Tzolk'in round in the womb.

- Our body has ten fingers and ten toes, which, multiplied by our thirteen major joints, equals 260. The 13 major joints are the neck, shoulders, elbows, wrists, hips, knees and ankles.

I believe that the Tzolk'in Clock also explains how human minds work. Looking at the whole Tzolk'in Clock, shown on the next page, the east face is where thoughts begin. In the center are three choices: accept, reject, or ignore. The west face is where the collective consciousness gives us guidance for our choices (labeled "Morals" here). The north face represents our right brain and the south face represents our left brain. I have drawn a blue arrow to show how thoughts pass through the Tzolk'in Clock (perhaps, a map of the human mind which resides on the inside of your third eye), from the origin of the thought to your choice on the thought, and how your morals guide your choices.

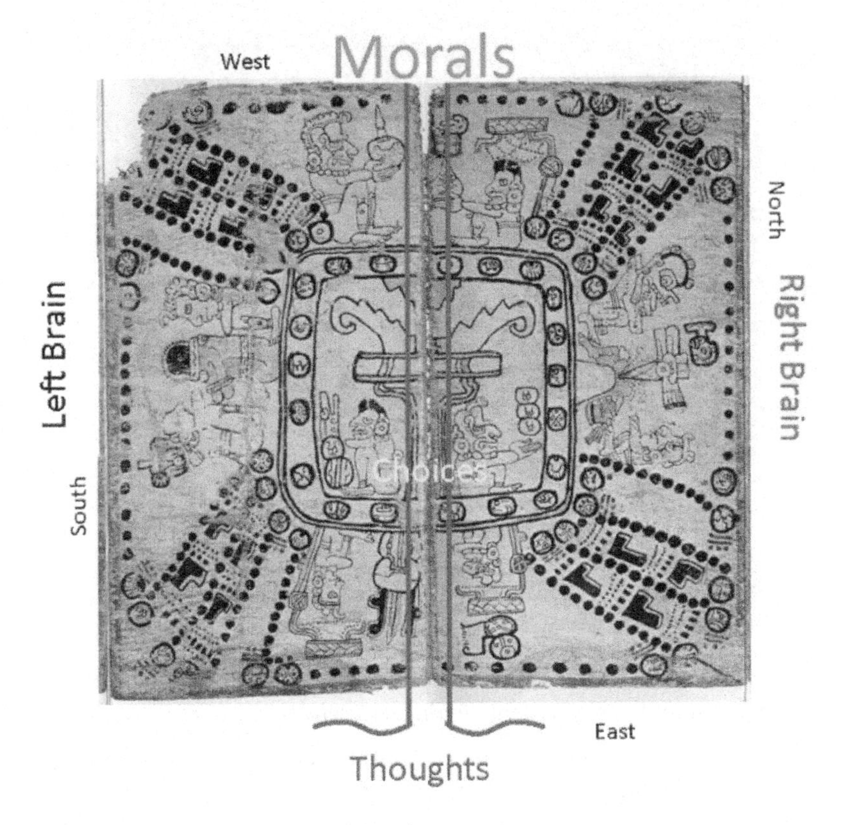

My research has shown the following patterns:

- People born on the morals side (team west) are good at managing other people.
- People born on the left-brain side (team south) are good at math, language, and logic.
- People born on the side where thoughts originate (team east) help others get along with each other.

- People born on the right-brain side (team north) are good at artistic expression.

Below is a picture from an ancient house in Tonina in which upside down Ik' windows connect underground rooms; where the wind blows intention into the seed. There are many T-shaped windows and doors found in southern Mexico, Guatemala, Belize and even in Arizona.

Here's how each day's energy connects on the Wind trecena. It's important to feel the shift of the day's energy during a trecena.

Each trecena has an ending direction. The Wind trecena ends on 13-Jaguar. It starts with 1-Wind, or, the breath of God, followed by 2-House which has the Ik' (Wind) shaped windows to allow the wind to pass through the house. The 3-Seed day is to conceive, in the house, seeds to be planted the next day. The 4-Serpent energy is like a new plant sprouting from the ground. The next day is the 5-Transformer with the energy of a caterpillar to a butterfly, a tadpole to a frog, a seed to a flower. Then it's almighty 6-Deer day pulling you from the underworld. Followed by the 7-Star day, when our star, Venus, rises above earth.

In other words, following a 5-Transformer day, it takes the sturdy foundation of 6-Deer to pull us out of the transformation energy. We've just spent the transformer day with our ancestors and it's time to get back to reality. Take what you have learned on 5-Transformer and apply it on 6-Deer. The next day is Venus, or Star. 7-Star is the day to look up to the sky and imagine great things that you can do.

8-Water has heavy undercurrents. Question everything and pay attention to what is happening around you. Be here right now and enjoy your day, even with the turbulence.

9-Dog is an aggressive morning energy followed by a dog day afternoon. Dog days are a wild card of the Tzolk'in. If you were born on any day with the inflection of 9, then 9-Dog is especially enjoyable.

10-Monkey is the day of choices and opportunities. Which road will you travel?

11-Road has lovely morning energy. Spend time remembering last night's dreams. Enjoy being alive and the feeling of being regenerated and fresh.

12-Reed is the day to feel God's love in your heart. Rejoice being connected to our creator.

13-Jaguar has morning energy filled with ying & yang. Focus on changes from slavery to freedom, and from fear to love. Connect with your natural self.

EAGLE

The Eagle trecena on the Tzolk'in Clock should be discussed together with the following Star trecena. They both play a more active role, working more closely together than the previous three trecenas. Shown below are these two trecenas as depicted in the Aztec version of the Tzolk'in. When folded upright in 3D, this would be on the southeast wall of an eight-sided room. The plant in the center of these two trecenas is fruiting. The parrot symbolizes the south. The Aztec version uses different symbols than the Maya version of the Tzolk'in. Rabbit in Aztec is Star in Maya, Vulture is Wisdom, Lizard is Seed, Grass is Road, and Flower is Sun. Notice 1-Rabbit (also known as Star, Venus, Lamat, and Q'anil) is prominently shown on the back of the parrot. 1-Rabbit is the hinge point of these two active trecenas, located on the southeast corner of the Tzolk'in Clock.

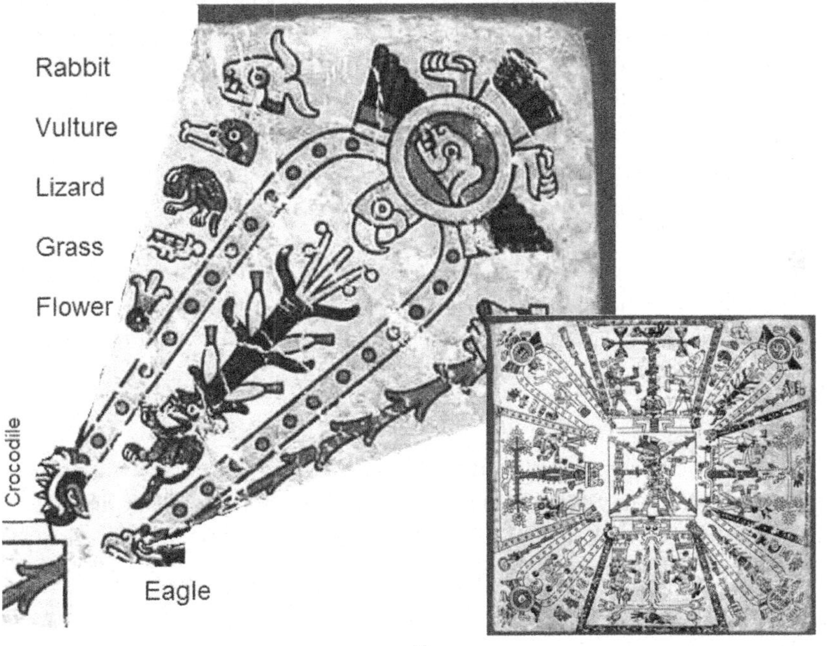

In the clip out above, you can see the eagle is starting the Eagle trecena. The rabbit is starting the Rabbit trecena. And, the crocodile is starting the new Tzolk'in round. In the smaller whole clip, you can see that the red beam from his head shows energy connecting to our throat chakra to the southeast corner of the Tzolk'in Clock. Various parts of the Tzolk'in Clock connect to a human (representing you) in the center of the Aztec version of the Tzolk'in.

The Tzolk'in Clock is multifaceted. One aspect is how to create your personal reality. After the Eagle and Rabbit trecenas is the Crocodile trecena —a time to plant news seeds of intentions that will become reality during the next Tzolk'in round. But before that time, these last two trecenas are about reaping our fruit from the past Tzolk'in round. The seeds we previously planted on the Crocodile trecena are now bearing fruit. The Tzolk'in Clock is a way to mentally plant seeds and properly nourish their growth into fruition. Now is the time to harvest your reality from the previous seed plantings. This is the advantage of knowing how to create your reality using the Tzolk'in Clock.

These next two trecenas are also a time of gratitude and sharing; a time of personal abundance and gracious acceptance. A time to give thanks to our creator, spiritual self, and personal self for our choices made this past Tzolk'in round. The Tzolk'in Clock is a tool that enables your ability to manifest your reality. Plant your wishes on 1-Crocodile, like planting a seed in your mental garden. Plant as many seeds as you can think, with loving packages that are decorated with art, in the fertile soil of the east. With these seeds, we have the power of our creator—our spiritual selves—and 260 days of time to assist in their manifestation. Take your well-prepared mental seeds, plant them, nurture them with the ebb and flow of 20 trecenas and create your personal reality. What seeds will you plant?

Also, be cautious when first using the Tzolk'in Clock. Don't fill your mental garden with too many seeds. As the Tzolk'in rounds pass, you will begin to learn how to expand your mental garden to plant more seeds. Again, these are like New Year's resolutions that are synchronistic with spiritual time.

Corner trecenas are more active than face trecenas. The previous three trecenas were firmly planted on the southern face of the Tzolk'in Clock. The energy from 1-Wisdom, 1-Water and 1-Wind has been building passively. During the next two trecenas, the southern energy will be actively released into our collective. People born during these next two trecenas tend to take action—like a player, rather than a coach. These two trecenas are about playing the game, doing the performance, or speaking out. People born on the southeast corner do this for all five trecenas of our southern Tzolk'in Clock energy.

1-Eagle	From sunset on13-Jaguar until sunrise on 1-Eagle, the first day of the eagle trecena meshes with the seventh day of the Water trecena. Today is the day to view your crops from above and decide which fruits you will harvest.
2-Wisdom	There are reasons that mental seeds bear fruit or do not bear fruit. Today is a good day to ponder your choices of this Tzolk'in round and learn better judgment of future choices.
3-Earth	Today is the day to examine the soil in your mind, where it is fertile, where it is poisoned. For instance, alcohol will ruin the fertile soil in certain areas of you mind / thoughts.
4-Flint	It's harvest time. Use the stability of the four directions as strength for tilling your soil today.
5-Storm	The wind will blow strong today. Use loving thoughts, loving intentions, and loving actions to cleanse your mind. Hug those you love. Resonate with your sacred love.
6-Ahau	Life enters your seeds today. These seeds are what you want to see as fruit, this time on the next Tzolk'in round.
7-Crocodile	Today is the day of emergence, on top of the pyramid energy of this trecena. It's the day to announce your intentions for the next Tzolk'in round (260 days), a tool to create your reality. (Note: Plants that didn't give fruit on their 1st Tzolk'in round may bear fruit on their 2nd or 3rd Tzolk'in round. It's like gardening in your mind. You can plant as many seeds as you want.)
8-Wind	a day to participate with our creator's blessing of our seeds for the next Tzolk'in round.

9-House	Today is a lovely energy, with fertile intention, as the sun rises in our house. It's a day to bless yesterday's intentions, in the comfort and safety of our house. It's a calming energy, as we prepare to receive our fruits from our previous seeds and prepare new seeds for planting.
10-Seed	Use your hands to prepare the ground for planting of your seeds. Collect the seeds from this Tzolk'in fruit to use on the next Tzolk'in round. Spread your fertile plants to fresh soil.
11-Serpent	There is a blend between your awake self and your consciousness when sleeping. Today is the day to get your spiritual self connected to your seeds, giving instructions to your spiritual self.
12-Transformer	Your seeds are now connected with your spiritual self. Spend time with your spiritual world. Think about your ancestors before you and your future generations ahead and our creator.
13-Deer	It's the end of the trecena. Today is the day to put the official seal of authority on the work you have done this trecena. It's the day to ask for protection of our mental / spiritual fields of crops.

Our next trecena is Star—a trecena of fertility.

STAR

The Star intention is also known as Rabbit, Venus, Lamat, and Q'anil. People born on Star days are naturally scribes and artists. This Star trecena is your time to write down intentions for the next Tzolk'in round. Where would you like to see your life 260 days from now? This is the time to write down instructions for your spiritual self to bring reality to your embodied self. The process of offering a seed to our spiritual self and receiving fruition is shown on the west and east faces of the Tzolk'in Clock.

West Face of the Tzolk'in clock

Awake self offering a seed to asleep self.

Asleep self accepting seed from awake self.

East Face of the Tzolk'in clock

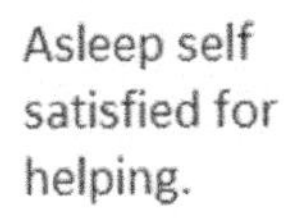

Awake self receiving from seed offered.

On the west face of the Tzolk'in Clock, your naked embodied self is making a request (planting a seed) of your spiritual self. On the east face of the Tzolk'in Clock, you're covered embodied self is receiving the requests from your spiritual self. In the center of the Tzolk'in Clock we see choices and decisions. As thoughts stream through your mind, from the east to the west, you choose to accept, reject or ignore. This process is depicted in the center of the Tzolk'in Clock, as shown in the Madrid codex.

Collectively, let's plant a seed for the next Tzolk'in round. This is a special Tzolk'in round for all of us. This is a time for people of all four directions to reunite with peace and love. Let's collectively decorate and plant a seed filled with peace and love in order to bring loving people to you.

New Years Day and Birthdays

Days on the Tzolk'in have spiritual energies that are not offered on the Gregorian calendar. It's interesting how many New Year's resolutions fail. I believe they fail because when we do them that way, we are doing them all by ourselves. On the Tzolk'in Clock, planting seeds on the first day allows your spiritual self to assist you. Tend to your seeds following the energy of each of the days listed for each of the 20 trecenas, so your seeds come to fruition.

Also, birthdays have spiritual meanings, so making a birthday wish really connects with our collective energy. Since the day's energy resonates with your energy on the Tzolk'in Clock, your wish flows into our collective energy. It's also a reason that people naturally want to gather around you and celebrate the day's energy. Being around people on their Tzolk'in birthday brings you closer to the day's energy.

Not all seeds planted come to fruition on the first Tzolk'in round. Like plants, they may take more than one Tzolk'in round to bear fruit. It's important to take care of the whole garden in your mind.

This may be your first time to use the Tzolk'in Clock. It's similar to saying a prayer, but with the idea that the prayer is a seed to nurture during each of the 20 trecenas of the 260-day Tzolk'in Clock.

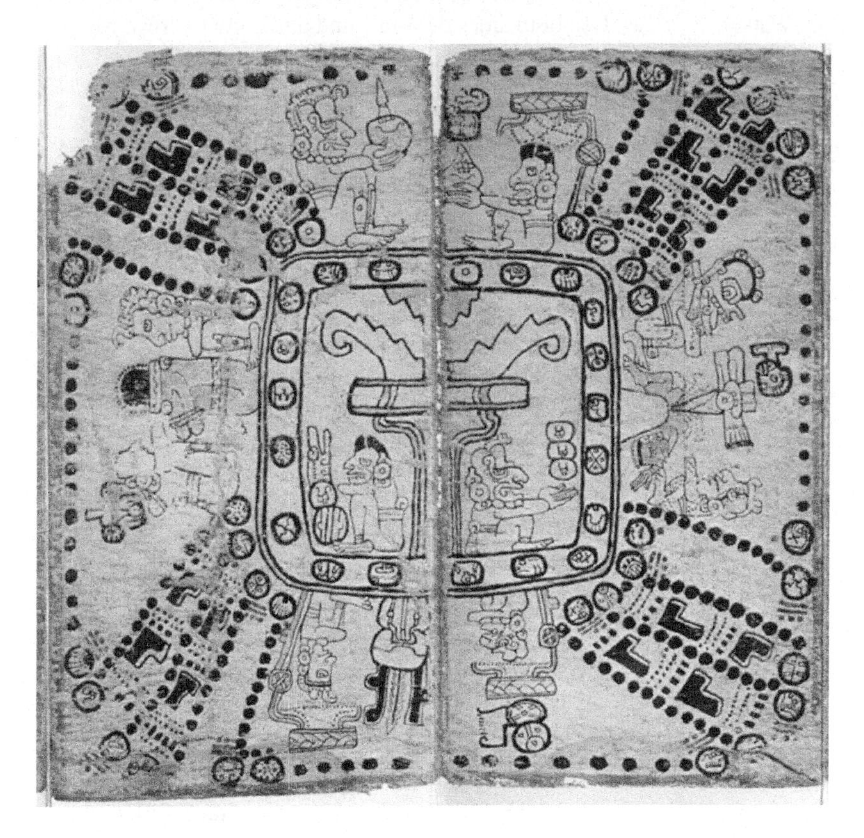

1-Star	This is a day to contemplate this whole trecena. This is a waiting day for the ride to begin. It is a time to shoot for the stars with dreams, hopes, and goals. You know you have the support of your creator, your spiritual self, and time of the Tzolk'in Clock.
2-Water	Your trecena journey begins as 1 star wanes and 2 water rises. Use both sides of your mind and body to "row, row, row your boat, gently down the stream."
3-Dog	This morning starts out energetic and the afternoon is lazy. At night, feel the monkey energy beginning.
4-Monkey	This is a playful day, filled with choices of which roads to travel on the next day.
5-Road	This is the day to decorate your seeds to be planted for the next Tzolk'in round. Sit at a desk today, and write down clear instructions, for your spiritual self to help create your new reality during this next Tzolk'in round. It's the power of 5 Road that will assist your writing, using the five fingers of your writing hand.
6-Reed	You have written, drawn, and decorated all your seeds for the next Tzolk'in. Today is the day to let your creator know about them. Meditate.
7-Jaguar	Your work is done. Walk through life knowing mother earth will provide all that you need.
8-Eagle	Visualize the next Tzolk'in round. Where will you be 260 days from today?
9-Wisdom	This is a day of confidence. It's a day to be proud of our accomplishments from the past Tzolk'in round, and proud of our decorations on our new seeds, to be planted.
10-Earth	This can be a very, very challenging day. The past Tzolk'in round is ending and the new Tzolk'in round is emerging. Use all ten toes and all ten fingers to brace yourself.
11-Flint	Today is the day of the "big" mirror. Look at yourself. What would you change to make yourself better? Cut out anything you don't like and make room for new seeds. It's also a day for tilling the soil. Metaphorically, use sharpened flint to till the fertile soil in your mind.

12-Storm	As 12 Storm builds up energy to blow away the dust left over from yesterday, feel the cleansing winds blowing through, cleansing your consciousness.
13-Light	It is equivalent to New Years Eve on the Gregorian calendar. It is a time to celebrate life.

CROCIDILE

Happy New Year! Creating and planting your seeds leads to awareness of the fertile ground. This trecena is about shaping the landscape of your mind, heart and spirit. Use the emergence of the crocodile trecena to strengthen your intentions.

These next three trecenas, on the east face of the Tzolk'in, surround the place where thoughts enter your mind.

Humans are creative and this trecena is a celebration of that. Thoughts become ideas that become reality. Inventions, art, and music get their inspiration from human thought.

The east face of the Tzolk'in would go around the door that faces east in a Navajo hoogan with eight sides. This is the beginning of the east face of the Tzolk'in Clock. These next three trecenas surround the entry of thought into your mind, heart and spirit. This is the time to meditate on your intentions for this new Tzolk'in round. This is the trecena to offer your new seeds of intention to our collective consciousness.

The seven days and six nights of a trecena relates to our seven chakras too. The Tzolk'in is a personal, human calendar. It is multi-dimensional and carries our collective consciousness through time.

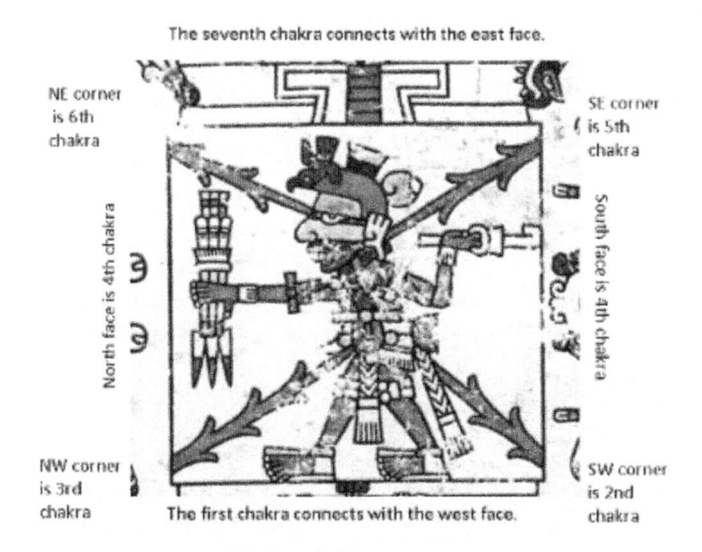

The human depicted in the center of the Aztec version of the Tzolk'in Clock, shows energy of the second, third, fifth, and sixth chakras. Each of these energies connects to one of the corners of the Tzolk'in Clock. The feet, heart and head connect to the first, fourth and seventh chakras, respectively.

The Crocodile trecena is on the crown chakra. This is just one of many humanistic qualities of the Tzolk'in Clock. Thoughts are received through our crown chakra and processed through our heart chakra using the balance of our feet (grounding) chakra. As this Tzolk'in Clock manifests your seeds of thought into reality, it must pass through the humanistic chakra energies. This gives life to our Tzolk'in round, as it connects our awake self with our spiritual self and our creator.

The day you were born has an assigned chakra that is more prevalent than the others. It's easy to spend too much energy focused on your birth chakra and that will lead to unbalance. I once asked a family of Mazatec shamans how to make my heart chakra larger and they said my heart chakra is fine, but my birth chakra is too large. Learn which chakra energy points at your Tzolk'in birthday and use it to benefit yourself and others. The goal is to balance all seven of your chakras and it helps to know how your chakra is connected to the Tzolk'in Clock.

The Tzolk'in Clock is embedded in the Aztec sun calendar (which has been misrepresented in much of modern western culture). The face in the center is not a blood thirsty sun. The face in the center is mother earth and she is speaking to us. She is speaking the message of the Tzolk'in to you right now. The sun is not speaking. It is hidden as an eagle, which flies above us. You can see the eagle in the center of this calendar, with its beak on top, claws on the side and feathers on the bottom. The sun flies over earth like an eagle. This YouTube video goes into excellent detail: https://youtu.be/0b9vqrjK2lQ

Your Tzolk'in Birthday

Imagine living with the Maya around 800AD in the late classic period. People born on the day's intention would be part of the day's ceremonies. If today was 1-Crocodile, then all people born on 1-Crocodile would gather at the temple. They would be available for others to ask questions and discuss the day's energy. Elders, who received 1-Crocodile as their new outlook, would also be included. People born with the first inflection of the trecena would stay at the temple for the entire trecena and be involved with special ceremonies day and night.

Imagine harnessing the power of your awake self, asleep self and our creator, and applying it collectively as a people. You can create reality! Imagine if hundreds and thousands of people were working together to create their collective reality, using the Tzolk'in Clock. Collectively planting seeds yields greater abundance than individual planting.

A profound Hopi prophecy exists saying this is the time for the re-unification of people from east, west, north and south. The Tzolk'in Clock is the center of all four directions. It's the genetic code of time and it is currently rebirthing. The Tzolk'in is a beacon for all to follow. It's about peace and love and understanding our creator of this physical realm and time. This calendar does not discriminate and includes everyone.

1-Crocodile	It's the eyes of the crocodile that sees above the water while its body is immersed in water. This is the energy of emergence.
2-Wind	It's the breath of our creator. It's the duality of thoughts and choices.
3-House	Take the energy of Wind and place in your heart (House) for your intention.
4-Seed	Your intention is ready for your spiritual self to receive.
5-Serpent	The energy of life is given to your seed, to grow into your reality, with the help of your creator, spiritual self, and the Tzolk'in Clock.
6-Transformer	Your seeds are now with your spiritual self.
7-Deer	The stability of the Deer intention brings you fully into your awake self. Immerse yourself in nature.
8-Star	Immerse yourself in the sky, the sun, moon, and wandering stars.
9-Water	Your internal waters are flowing. Shape the path of your water to improve your soil. Take control of your energies.
10-Dog	This is a fun day. It's a day to use your 10 fingers to make music and ten toes to dance. Your rocks have been lifted; today is the day to let them roll. If your inflection is 10, this is your Dog day, too.
11-Monkey	It's time to think again. You've seen your fields, you've planted your crops, and your spiritual self is aware. Think about where to place your energy.
12-Road	Today is the abundance of grass. You can walk all over grass, yet it grows and grows. Appreciate all your landscape, give yourself blessings.
13-Reed	Feel God appreciate you. Our purpose is love and God shows his appreciation for you today. Rest, relax, and feel the love within you.

JAGUAR

The Tzolk'in relates to many aspects of our human experience. One of these aspects is the human mind. We have a left and right side of our brain. The left side of your brain controls the right side of your body, and vice versa. Your corpus callosum is the connection between the left and right side of your brain.

The Jaguar trecena on the east face of the Mayan Tzolk'in calendar crossing south to north.

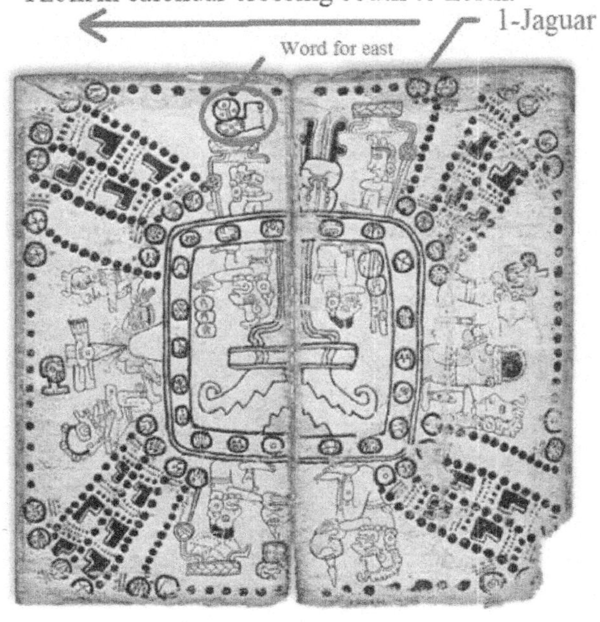

Just like your brain, the Tzolk'in Clock also has a left (north) and right (south) side. As the energy moves from south to north, it crosses the centerline from 7-Ahau to 8-Crocodile of this trecena. Halfway around the

Tzolk'in Clock (130 days later) it crosses from the north side to the south side on 7-Dog to 8-Monkey on the Seed trecena.

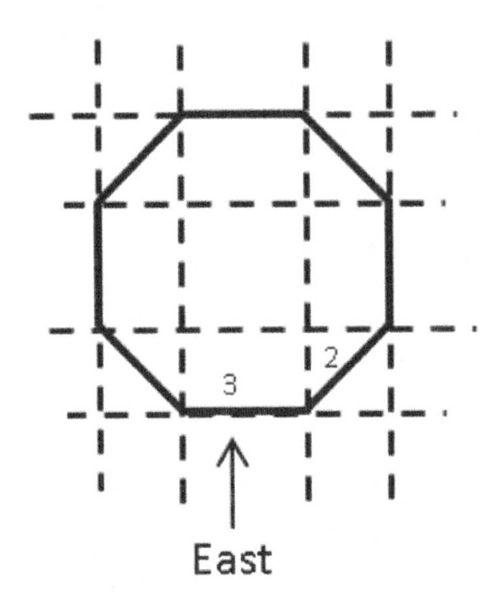

The south side is equivalent to the left brain and the north side is equivalent to the right brain. The north side starts with 1-Transformer and the south side starts with 1-Wisdom. This relates to the wisdom, or logic side, of the left brain and the imagination, or dream state, of the right brain.

Every 260 days the cycle repeats. This is how the 3D version of the Tzolk'in Clock frames your mind.

There are ball courts in the Navajo nation. Both the Navajo and Maya have twin heroes. Maya chocolate has been found in New Mexico at Chaco Canyon. What if the Navajo people had the imagination to make their sacred home in the shape of the Tzolk'in Clock? And, the Navajo hoogan is shaped identical to the Tzolk'in Clock, which has the same three-trecena, two- trecena pattern.

The dimensions of a hoogan are identical to the Tzolk'in. The east, west, south and north faces have three lengths and the corners have two lengths. The faces of the Tzolk'in have three trecenas, and the corners have two trecenas. The door to the hoogan faces east. If viewed in 3D, the Jaguar trecena would go across and above the door to the hoogan. This is where the light shines into the hoogan as the sun rises in the east. If viewed in 3D in your mind, this is where thoughts enter your mind. Also, your internal flame is the cast iron furnace in the center of the hoogan, just as shown in the Madrid version of the Tzolk'in.

Dr. Carl Calleman goes into detail about the eight partitions of the human mind in his book "The Mind and the Rise of Civilization". He even references this very topic in that book.

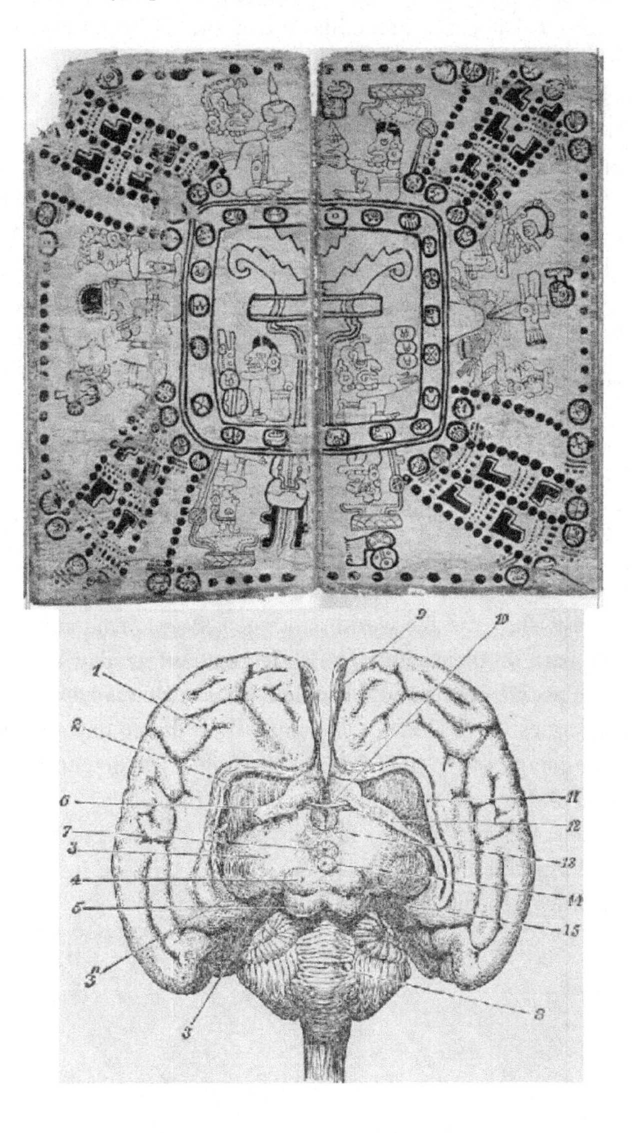

There is a noted difference between face people and corner people. Corner people stir things up. It's their nature to do this. Face people don't have that power. Yet, the way the trecena pattern works, the face people rely on the corner people to have their intentions offered to the collective consciousness. When the energy begins on 1-Crocodile, the energy of the past five trecenas ended on 13-Light. The entire south side of the Tzolk'in Clock goes dark. Its intention has been fulfilled. On 1-Crocodile the entire east face and corner of the Tzolk'in Clock lights up. The energy builds from 1-Crocodile to 2-Wind to 3-Night to 4-Seed, etc. This energy builds up through the trecena. On 1-Crocodile, all of the 1-Crocodile people pour their intentions into the collective consciousness. And the next day it builds to 2-Wind. And builds and builds until 13-Reed. That day begins a higher trecena. It starts on 1-Jaguar and builds until 13-Transformer. That day begins on 1-Deer, the third trecena on the front face. After that trecena, begins 1-Light. 1-Light is the first day of a corner trecena. The corners not only pour their intentions into the collective consciousness, they flow like a flag or a spoon. The corners spray the intentions that started with three-face trecenas into the collective consciousness, like seeds from a flower. The two 7 days (7-Transformer and 7-Storm) are especially free to spray their intentions of the entire three-trecena face and two-trecena corner into the collective consciousness. And then after 13-Serpent, the entire face and corner go dark. It is time for the north face and corner to do their work, starting on 1-Transformer.

Timing the Tzolk'in Clock

Your birthday day is the day to let the world know your intentions—the day you "make a wish." And the world will listen. People naturally want to be with people born on their day. You also learn about the day's energy when being around people on their day. People born at night may take on either of the day's energies. Here is how the change from day to day occurs: As the sun sets, the energy of the next day will emerge. At midnight, the levels of energy cross. As the sun rises, only the energy of that day will be present. As the sun sets, the energy of the next day gradually emerges. Both energies are shared during the night. People born at night will feel which energy is right for them; which energy was in their first breath.

1-Jaguar	The Jaguar energy gets its own trecena. And, like a cat walking over a doorway, this trecena walks over the doorway of the east face.
2-Eagle	Try to stay focused today. Share who you are with a friend. Use the height of an eagle and both eyes to view your spiritual landscape.
3-Wisdom	After viewing yourself, you have new wisdom. Let it sink into yourself.
4-Earth	Where is your flint? Today is the day to find the tools you need to shape the landscape of yourself.
5-Flint	Today is the day to look inside and decide what you want to remove. Similar to gardening, today is the day to trim.
6-Storm	Your spiritual wind is blowing into your mind to feed the furnace of your soul and keep your flame alive.
7-Light	Today is a rebirthing experience. All of the darkness removed on 5-Flint and swept away by 6-Storm is now raw and bare and ready to receive light for new growth. Shine light on the seeds that you planted this Tzolk'in round. Contemplate their fruition today. Take a walk to free your mind's creativity. Your mind is your sanctuary and walking brings calmness, placid waters, and union with God.
8-Crocodile	We have collectively crossed from the left side to the right side of the Tzolk'in Clock. When the currents of life are swift, use the strength and stability of Crocodile. Look out with your eyes for messages today.
9-Wind	Your new intentions will bring your thoughts/seeds into reality. Your mind is fertile soil in which new ideas, seeds and plants form your reality.
10-House	With ten fingers and ten toes, it is a good day to work around your house, your mind, your body, and your senses with Jaguar energy.

11-Seed	Your reality is being affected now. Be aware of situations that change your way, such as something breaking so you end up somewhere else and meet someone special. These are the days to be thankful.
12-Serpent	This is a day of social awareness and our connections with others.
13-Transformer	It's a lovely energy today. There's calmness to it. It’s a “Sunday” on the trecena. As the sun sets tonight, the energy of 1-Deer begins.

DEER

The deer trecena uses an energy of stamping something with authority. Who are you with authority? There is no room for doubt. It's knowing you are right and knowing you are wrong.

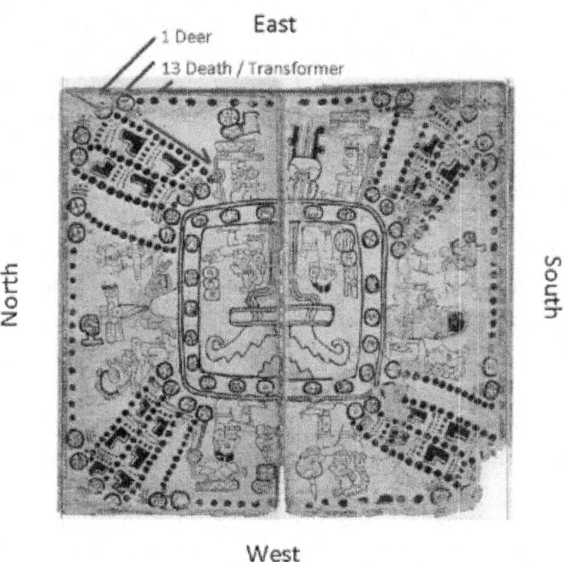

The previous Jaguar trecena crossed the top of the east face of the Tzolk'in Clock (shown). The Deer trecena travels down along the north side of the east face. The next two trecenas (Light and Reed) are on the east to north corner of the Tzolk'in Clock.

People born on deer days should realize that not all people are like you. You need to temper your judgment, because you have the power to drop the hammer. People born on the other day intentions are not given the Deer role of authority.

It's also a day of giving authority to others. *Yes, I can do this!* So, your role is also supportive; as if giving people the seal of approval to be themselves. People need this. It helps them eliminate doubt from their goals. Deer people can build people up or tear them down with ease.

The Deer trecena also connects us closely to nature, especially using our five physical senses plus our Deer sense. It's our time to use the medicines that nature has to offer. Deer represents our collective morals. It is also the energy that brings us out of our sleep after the previous day's Transformer energy. Deer energy peacefully reconnects our spirit to earth and body by pulling us out of our sleep state of the collective consciousness.

Your Elder Intention

After 52 Ha'ab years on the Tzolk'in and Ha'ab calendars a person has experienced every combination of days possible. When this cycle completes there is an eight-day gap between the stars in the sky and Tzolk'in. Based on that eight-day gap, you get a new outlook on life, commonly referred to as "your mid-life crisis." However, it's not a crisis—it's enlightenment. You have seen the past 52 Ha'ab years through one outlook. When you turn 52-years-old, you get a new outlook, and your vision of life is improved from monocular to bi-ocular.

Consider each dot shown on the Tzolk'in as a different outlook. It's very rare that two people born on the same Tzolk'in day get to interact. The odds are 1:260. This helps explain how people are always seeing the same things differently. Yet, our collective consciousness sees all 260 outlooks at once. The Tzolk'in Clock is a map of our collective interactions. Once you map your family and friends and co-workers on the Tzolk'in Clock you will better understand their points of view.

There is also a special relationship on the Tzolk'in Clock for two people born on directly opposite days. When folded into a 3D view, each of the 260 outlooks points directly at one of the other outlooks. How would these two people interact? Could this be a "soulmate" interaction? Would they have "telepathic" communication? My research has found three long and successful marriages born on the opposite trecena.

The connection is deeper. More than having things in common. It's an energy connection of all seven chakras. You can easily see a soulmates point of view as if in their mind while they see their own thoughts.

Could there be a special combination of four people on the Tzolk'in when interacting? Could they collectively achieve a higher collective state of mind? Could they collectively get a better view on ideas that matter to the public? Gathering people and mapping their locations on the Tzolk'in Clock and discussing ideas would offer an opportunity for many group experiments. For instance, asking for a social solution from four people born on 1-Reed, 1-Flint, 1-Night and 1-Star might give a better collective solution for all of us. It would be a well rounded and represented solution with perspectives from all four directions.

The Deer Elder

The Deer was a Rainstorm before she was born. Her Deer spirit was born 52 years after her body was formed. As she waited to become a deer, she pondered. She has a deep understanding of mother earth and she can create rainstorms at will. She sees all of creation does not yet have a voice to share her understandings. Still a mere Rainstorm, she expressed herself openly and honestly.

A Sheet for Your Use

The following sheet lists all 260 Tzolk'in days as they flow from east, north, west and south. The first row is the east face of the Tzolk'in Clock starting with 1-Crocodile. The second row is the north face starting with 1-Transformer. The third row is the west face starting with 1-Monkey. The forth row is the south starting with 1-Wisdom.

You can use this to mark your friends and family. It helps to remember or share their Tzolk'in birthdays.

Each row is a team. Team East, Team North, Team West and Team East. People born on the same team tend to get along, naturally. See if you can locate 6-Storm and 9-Rabbit. Which team are they on? Which team are you on? Are any of your friends on the same team as you?

	1 Croc	1 jaguar	1 deer	1 sun	1 reed
	2 wind	2 eagle	2 star	2 Croc	2 jaguar
	3 night	3 wisdom	3 offering	3 wind	3 eagle
	4 seed	4 earth	4 dog	4 night	4 wisdom
	5 serpent	5 flint	5 monkey	5 seed	5 earth
	6 transformer	6 storm	6 road	6 serpent	6 flint
Team East	7 deer	7 sun	7 reed	7 transformer	7 storm
	8 star	8 Croc	8 jaguar	8 deer	8 sun
	9 offering	9 wind	9 eagle	9 star	9 Croc
	10 dog	10 night	10 wisdom	10 offering	10 wind
	11 monkey	11 seed	11 earth	11 dog	11 night
	12 road	12 serpent	12 flint	12 monkey	12 seed
	13 reed	13 transformer	13 storm	13 road	13 serpent
	1 transformer	1 storm	1 road	1 serpent	1 flint
	2 deer	2 sun	2 reed	2 transformer	2 storm
	3 star	3 Croc	3 jaguar	3 deer	3 sun
	4 offering	4 wind	4 eagle	4 star	4 Croc
	5 dog	5 night	5 wisdom	5 offering	5 wind
	6 monkey	6 seed	6 earth	6 dog	6 night
Team North	7 road	7 serpent	7 flint	7 monkey	7 seed
	8 reed	8 transformer	8 storm	8 road	8 serpent
	9 jaguar	9 deer	9 sun	9 reed	9 transformer
	10 eagle	10 star	10 Croc	10 jaguar	10 deer
	11 wisdom	11 offering	11 wind	11 eagle	11 star
	12 earth	12 dog	12 night	12 wisdom	12 offering
	13 flint	13 monkey	13 seed	13 earth	13 dog
	1 monkey	1 seed	1 earth	1 dog	1 night
	2 road	2 serpent	2 flint	2 monkey	2 seed
	3 reed	3 transformer	3 storm	3 road	3 serpent
	4 jaguar	4 deer	4 sun	4 reed	4 transformer
	5 eagle	5 star	5 Croc	5 jaguar	5 deer
	6 wisdom	6 offering	6 wind	6 eagle	6 star
Team West	7 earth	7 dog	7 night	7 wisdom	7 offering
	8 flint	8 monkey	8 seed	8 earth	8 dog
	9 storm	9 road	9 serpent	9 flint	9 monkey
	10 sun	10 reed	10 transformer	10 storm	10 road
	11 Croc	11 jaguar	11 deer	11 sun	11 reed
	12 wind	12 eagle	12 star	12 Croc	12 jaguar
	13 night	13 wisdom	13 offering	13 wind	13 eagle
	1 wisdom	1 offering	1 wind	1 eagle	1 star
	2 earth	2 dog	2 night	2 wisdom	2 offering
	3 flint	3 monkey	3 seed	3 earth	3 dog
	4 storm	4 road	4 serpent	4 flint	4 monkey
	5 sun	5 reed	5 transformer	5 storm	5 road
	6 Croc	6 jaguar	6 deer	6 sun	6 reed
Team South	7 wind	7 eagle	7 star	7 Croc	7 jaguar
	8 night	8 wisdom	8 offering	8 wind	8 eagle
	9 seed	9 earth	9 dog	9 night	9 wisdom
	10 serpent	10 flint	10 monkey	10 seed	10 earth
	11 transformer	11 storm	11 road	11 serpent	11 flint
	12 deer	12 sun	12 reed	12 transformer	12 storm
	13 star	13 Croc	13 jaguar	13 deer	13 sun

1-Deer	Watch yourself this trecena and avoid getting yourself into trouble with the authorities. Sync yourself with natural law and stay present with nature.
2-Star	Focus on your goals. Find new places in your mental fields to plant new seeds.
3-Water	Today's energy can toss you around. Hang out with your family and friends for support. Offer your prayers to flowing water.
4-Dog	This is seriously a dog day afternoon. It's a fun day at the dog park.
5-Monkey	It's a playful day. Monkey days are the day of choices for tomorrow (6-Road). Which road should you take to travel? 4/20
6-Road	A fun day for short trips and appreciating others.
7-Reed	Today's energy is the human connection to God. Where does God connect with you? Feel the graceful energy of mother earth and father sky.
8-Jaguar	Get in touch with your animal side. Get frisky.
9-Eagle	As the eagle flies high in the energy of 9.
10-Wisdom	Try something new, like counting the number of smiles you give to other people.
11-Earth	This day especially connects with the Deer trecena. Feel how the day's energy changes from 10-Wisdom to 11-Earth and from 11-Earth to 12-Flint.
12-Flint	Today is the day for deep introspection, and the opportunity to remove those core areas inside of you that bother you. Use the mirror of the obsidian stone to see, and the sharp edges to cut and remove. 13-Storm will blow away all those clippings.
13-Storm	As the sun sets, the energy of 1-Ahau will begin. This will be a trecena of new light on areas previously hidden. Make room in the garden of your mind for new growth. Ahau days are also days we connect with our ancestors. This is the undertone for the next 13 days.

SUN (OR, FLOWER)

The sun and reed trecenas are shown in the Madrid and Fejervary codices (below). These two trecenas are between the east and north faces of the Tzolk'in Clock. Previous articles discussed the human mind aspect of the Tzolk'in calendar as well as planting seeds on 1-Crocodile. The center of the Fejervary depiction shows a bird taking a seed from a flower. It is during these two trecenas that our seeds are being collected by our collective consciousness, the place of our consciousness when we go to sleep. These two trecenas are a transition from the east face of the Tzolk'in Clock to the north face. The north face of the Tzolk'in Clock begins with 1-Transformer, which is shown as a skull below.

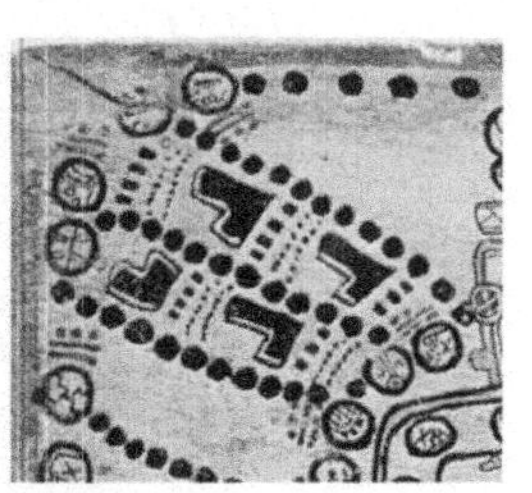

Above is the Mayan Madrid codex of the Tzolk'in clock, showing the Light trecena and the Reed trecena on the east-north corner of the Tzok'in clock.

Left is the Aztec Fejervary codex of the Tzolk'in clock.

This trecena begins as shown with 1-Flower.

The next trecena begins as shown with 1-Reed. (top left)

The next trecena begins as shown with 1-Death

This is just one of several articles discussing the Tzolk'in Clock's interactions with all our humanistic experiences. The Tzolk'in Clock should be viewed in 3D with you in the center. It would be like sitting in a Navajo hoogan and having each of the eight walls painted with a face or corner of the Tzolk'in Clock. The doorway to the hoogan faces east. We have just completed the east face, and we are beginning the east-north corner of the Tzolk'in Clock. The north face is the veil between your awake self and your asleep self—your conscious enslaved self and your freed unconscious self. The north face of the Tzolk'in Clock is like the right brain of a human.

But before we start the north face of the Tzolk'in Clock, we must time travel through the east-north corner, beginning on 1-Sun (or, 1-Flower) and ending after the Reed trecena on 13-Serpent. The two trecenas in the northeast corner of the Tzolk'in Clock are a time to enjoy the landscape of your mind, heart, soul, as well as others who are going through this same time as our collective equivalents.

Two artists replicated the Madrid codex version of the Tzolk'in. The Maya had nunneries that taught about our physical spirit and our sleep spirit (Nawal). The south face of the Tzolk'in Clock (next to Ed) shows a human enslaved. The north face of the Tzolk'in Clock (next to Lisa) shows a human being freed from his consciousness. The joining and separation of consciousness from awake to asleep begins at birth and takes place every time you sleep until at death.

The Sun (Ahau) trecena begins just below Lisa's hand. You can see the Ahau symbol. Each of the dots, traveling from her hand to her belt, represents a day of the Sun trecena.

It's also interesting that trecenas have day days and night days, but the Gregorian week only has day days. So, on the Gregorian calendar is always mon*day*, tues*day*, wednes*day*, thurs*day*, fri*day* and even on weekends it's satur*day* and sun*day*. The trecena gives you six nights between seven days. 1-Sun is the first day of this trecena. 2-Crocodile is the first night. 3-Wind is the second day. And so on.

The Tzolk'in Clock is the generating force for all other calendars (Ha'ab, Tun, Venus, etc.). Our collective energy builds and builds through the trecena, until it has enough energy to jump to the next trecena. You can tune your activities with this natural energy. The Tzolk'in is our spiritual time and earth is our spiritual place.

For example, if you had a project that would take about 2 weeks to complete, you could gradually begin your project on the first day of a trecena. Then, you can take a rest from it on the second day. On the third day, you put much more work into it and then rest on the fourth day. On the seventh day ("hump day") on the trecena, you should be at maximum effort. By that day, most of the hard work is completed, but you still have the rest of the trecena to complete the project. So, later in the trecena, you are simply tying up loose ends to complete the project, and the effort isn't nearly as difficult. By the thirteenth day (the end of the trecena) you should have finished, and it's a day to relax and get ready for the next trecena.

It's very doubtful that any Mesoamerican culture separated a day into 24 hours. I believe that a day's energy begins at sunset, lasts the next day and ends the next sunrise. That's about 36 hours. Dividing that by 13 sections gives roughly 2.8 hours of time. It is possible that daily energies also ebb and flow like a trecena. The maximum flow each day's energy lasts for 2.8 hours when the sun is highest in the sky (±1.4 hours). If true, then each day's energy would flow like this.

Sunset is the 1st wave. Midnight is the 3rd wave. Sunrise is the 5th wave. Noon is the 7th wave. Sunset is the 9th wave. Midnight is the 11th wave. And, sunrise is the 13th wave. It's at night that one days energy begins as the previous days energy ends. They overlap at night. It's only during the day time that the day's energy is not mixed with the previous or next day's energy.

1-Sun	Take time in the morning to enjoy the shift from deer to sun. Feel the refreshing breeze in a quiet environment. Enjoy this fresh Sun energy.
2-Crocodile	The seeds you planted 40 days ago, are ready to be received by your sleep-self and nourished for the next 130 days on the left side of the Tzolk'in Clock.
3-Wind	If your mind, heart and soul had curtains, today, they will be gently blowing.
4-House	Your physical self may feel weird today as your spiritual self uses the stability of 4 to take your seeds.
5-Seed	Spend time in the morning remembering your dreams. The veil between your awake and sleep self is slightly open. The dreams from last night will give glimpses of your future.
6-Serpent	The serpent energy generates waves of the energy for life to exist. It can also be a day of ups and downs.
7-Transformer	You can now envision the fruits of your seeds and see the "new" you beginning to take shape. You can sense energy from the north face of the Tzolk'in Clock in 20 days (on 1-Transformer).
8-Deer	"This is a day of great spiritual power and to sense where your personal powers lie." Jaguar Wisdom (last Tzolk'in round)
9-Star	The reason this day is so feminine and fertile, is its association with nine cycles of the moon, about the gestation cycle of a woman. Combine that with the energy of ripening corn, and you get the most fertile day of the Tzolk'in.
10-Water	Resonate with today's calm and placid waters.
11-Dog	This is an active energy day, with dog-like enthusiasm.
12-Monkey	This is a playful day, filled with possibilities. Today is known as the weaver of time, for tomorrow is 13-Road (Destiny). Today is the day to choose a path for the next 20 days.

13-Road	LOVE, as abundant as grass, is our purpose…and reason for being created. Enjoy the last day of the Sun trecena. As the sun sets tonight, the new Reed trecena energy begins to rise and things may get wild.

REED

The Reed trecena is that last trecena on the east side of the Tzolk'in Clock. After this trecena, the energy of the Tzolk'in is shifted to the north. The north face is the spiritual side of the Tzolk'in Clock. It is the place we go when we sleep and is equivalent to the right side of the human brain.

The Reed trecena celebrates our human qualities and the physical way we experience "god's handiwork." The Reed trecena's destination is on the last day of 13-Serpent. At the beginning of this trecena on 1-Reed, our animal energy (2-Jaguar) emerges from the reeds and jumps into the air, flying high as an eagle (3-Eagle), gaining wisdom (4-Wisdom), pouncing back, then landing on earth (5-Earth/Earthquake) with a quake, as the Transformer energy of the next trecena (1-Transformer) receives your seeds planted on the Crocodile trecena. This trecena involves transferring your intentions (seeds) from your thoughts to your sleep consciousness, where they will develop during the north face of the Tzolk'in Clock.

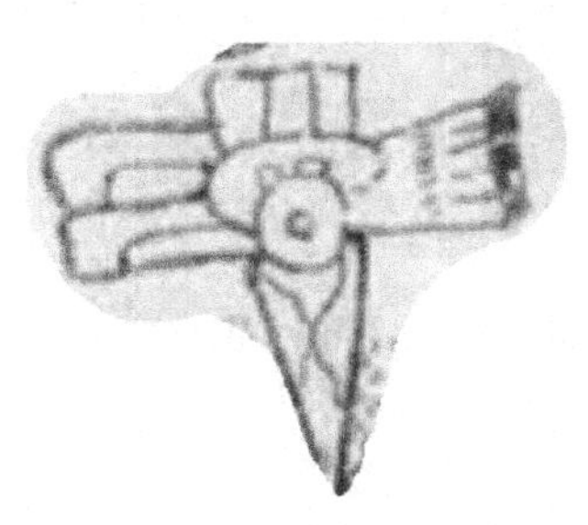

The middle of the Reed trecena is about finding spiritual tools (6-Flint) that fit your dominate hand to cleanse your heart when we travel through the north face of the Tzolk'in Clock. This image of a flint-like tool is the located at the center of the north face as depicted in the Madrid codex. You can see the tool fixed to the heart of the stylized bird. It's during the Reed trecena that you find your tools. It's during the north face, that the tools are used by your spiritual self to accept, cleanse and manifesting your seeds in the realm beyond our physical connection. During the east-north corner of the Tzolk'in Clock, your intentions emerge into your spiritual (sleep) consciousness and reality. Blessings are given to your seeds during the Reed trecena, as your awake self (thoughts) give them to your spiritual self. During the north face of the Tzolk'in Clock, your seeds are planted, watered and accepted as destiny by your spiritual self. This is the second step of the Tzolk'in Clock, going from east to north.

The Reed trecena is also about the energy that connects your life to a higher purpose. The Reed intention is the driving force of consciousness to experience life and love. The Tzolk'in is the timekeeper of this energy, letting us know when it occurs and how it occurs. To paraphrase Dr. Calleman's work, from a multi-cultural aspect, the Tzolk'in is the left-brain teachings, the eastern teachings are the right-brain versions, and the brain's corpus callosum is the yin and yang of the Middle East teachings.

The image above depicts the Reed intention: "God has put a sense of justice inside of all humans as a reflection of Himself." Cherish every moment and live in the moment (not with worry or regret) and love what is given to your reality.

This is a 260-day method to connect with our collective consciousness and manifest our requests. Relax with confidence, knowing your spiritual self has your intentions and will be actively working everyday on the Tzolk'in Clock.

Mapping the Tzolk'in Clock to Your Mind

Touch just above your right eyebrow, using your right hand. Go straight up to the top of your forehead. That's the Crocodile trecena. Now go across your forehead. That's the Jaguar trecena. Go down to your left eyebrow. That's the Deer trecena. All three of those trecenas are the east side of the Tzolk'in Clock. Now go up, over and down your left temple. Those are the Light (going up) and Reed (going down) trecenas. This pattern continues around your head. Go up and over and down your left ear. Those are the Transformer, Storm and Road trecenas. This pattern is repeated all around your head, ending downwards on your right temple with the Star trecena. Now find your location. That is your outlook. That is where the day's energy shines on your Maya Tzolk'in birthday.

This pattern maps the 260 different outlooks for each day of the Tzolk'in. This pattern is how so many people can see the same thing and get a completely different perspective. This is also why elders, having two outlooks, get a better perspective. Also, the interaction of your perspective to each day is different. For instance, you may love certain days on the Tzolk'in based on your perspective to it; whereas another person may not enjoy it as much. This is how we are collectively connected. The Tzolk'in connects in many ways to our human experience. Which is your perspective?

The East (3-Trecenas) Face and East-North (2-Trecenas) Corner of the Tzolk'in Clock

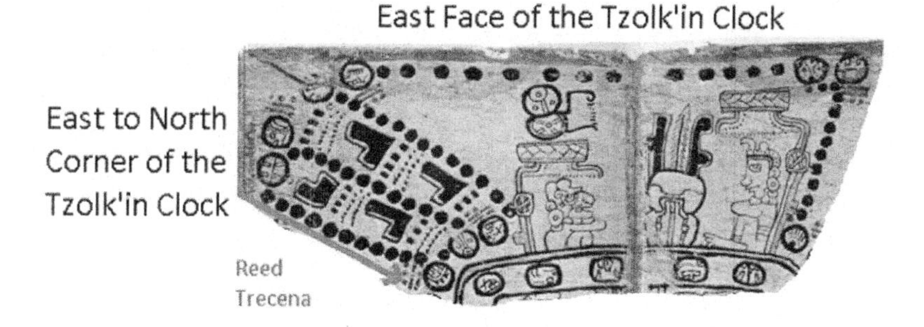

The east face began with 1-Crocodile. The Tzolk'in day energy is carried from the Crocodile trecena to the Jaguar trecena, then to the Deer trecena. The east face of the Tzolk'in Clock is stable and fixed in place. The stability of the face allows the two corner trecenas to whip, or flap, or disperse the east face energy. It's a natural way to release the energy into our collective consciousness. Statistically, 60 percent are born on a face and 40 percent are born on a corner. Personalities of face and corner people are different, as corner people tend to stir things up and face people tend to like more stability.

Imagine a rear screen light projected through this image. The light shines on the whole screen, but the point of light moves, day by day. The burden of the light is held by all 65 days of team east and that burden of time is lifted off their shoulders when the Reed trecena ends. Then the burden will be placed on people born on the north face and north-west corner (team north). When it is your Tzolk'in birthday, it is your responsibility to participate with our collective consciousness and you must also carry it for all five trecenas (65 days) with your team members.

1-Reed	The beginning of this trecena's energy is like laying in the forest, looking over a valley as the sun sets on the horizon. Nature is plush and comfortable to the touch and welcoming to walk through. A stream nearby brings out the forest animals, and the air is fresh.
2-Jaguar	A strong animal energy emerges today, like a Jaguar ready to pounce. Be aware to control this energy.
3-Eagle	Get a higher point of view on yourself today. Prepare your heart for some remodeling during the north face of the Tzolk'in Clock.
4-Wisdom	When something "bad" happens, it's only meant for you to find something better. Trust that the obstacles changing your path will take you to a better place.
5-Earth	After flying high on 3-Eagle and gaining 4-Wisdom, plunge your dominate hand into mother earth with force and grab your spiritual tools.
6-Flint	Today is a great day for inner reflection. Offer your spiritual tools to your heart energy with loving thoughts, words, and intentions.
7-Storm	Live the life that you are supposed to be living. This is the natural way. Trust that father sky will protect you and mother earth will provide for you.
8-Light	Life can be harsh. Hearing from others and sharing your words every day soothes some of the roughness, of it all.
9-Crocodile	Today is the day of emergence. Cherish and live in the moment without worry or regret. Appreciate your surroundings.
10-Wind	It takes wind to blow your seeds into the spiritual realm and the powerful inflection of 10 is there for you. Give blessings to your seeds. Blow your seeds from your hands into the spiritual realm where you sleep.
11-House	This morning's sunrise will be blissful. Go out this morning, face east and say prayers. Rejoice as the first rays of light touch you.

12 Seed	Your seeds are complete, and your spiritual self is ready to use them. It's a good day to take a nap for a refreshing deep sleep.
13 Serpent	Serpent days often have ups and downs, so be cautious. You are going to love how you feel at sunrise tomorrow. Appreciate everything that is going right for you.

TRANSFORMER

The Tzolk'in Clock should be viewed as though you are sitting in the center, facing east. The fire in the center is your Akbal. Each of the four corners and four faces folds up, so you are surrounded by eight walls, like in a hoogan. The front face is east, the back face is west. The Transformer trecena begins the north face of the Tzolk'in Clock, the left side of your mind, and your heart chakra. This trecena begins our travel around the veil of our awake self and asleep self (the place where our consciousness goes when we sleep) as we begin the north face of the Tzolk'in Clock.

The east face of the Tzolk'in Clock is about thought (Crocodile), the north face is about our right brain (Transformer), the west face is about collective morals (Monkey), and the south face is about our left brain (Wisdom). The Tzolk'in Clock is a way to transform our lives from "chasing the dollar" on the Gregorian calendar to "using your spiritual self to deliver your reality". Using the Tzolk'in Clock, you have your reality presented to you. Chasing materialistic wealth on the Gregorian calendar takes a lot of external energy. Creating your reality with spiritual time is done with your thoughts and consciousness surrounded by calm, placid water. So be mindful of how, when and where you choose to put your energy.

This trecena begins our journey into the left side of the mind (right side of the brain). There is no ego on this side of the Tzolk'in Clock. Each night, when we fall asleep our consciousness leaves the prison of our physical selves. It's during the north face of the Tzolk'in Clock that our spiritual selves work on the seeds we planted on the east face of the Tzolk'in Clock.

This is a good time to consider who is the ruler of our collective consciousness? Looking outward at human existence, is there something that could change? Do we have any control over our future generations? Every Tzolk'in round our collective consciousness is updated on 8-Monkey, on the west face of the Tzolk'in Clock. The Transformer trecena is a good time to remember our intentions set the previous 8-Monkey and prepare the next update.

The north face of the Tzolk'in Clock is when and where your individual spirits that make up your consciousness go their separate ways. They scatter your intentions into the collective consciousness like seeds in the wind. When you wake up each morning they return, the veil is closed, and your consciousness is again contained. Your awake self is back in control. The Tzolk'in Clock is all about using the collective consciousness to create your physical reality.

The north face of the Tzolk'in Clock is the time to weave your dreams into reality. With all of the power of our creator, imagine your reality as you want it to be. This is the time to build on the seeds that you planted on the east face of the Tzolk'in Clock. Use your intuition to know what can really become reality and focus your spiritual intentions on those fertile plants.

The north face of the Tzolk'in Clock starts with the Transformer intention. This is the cornerstone of the north face, just as Monkey is the cornerstone of the west face, Wisdom is the cornerstone of the south face, and Crocodile is the corner tone of the east face. The Transformer energy is carried throughout the north face and the northwest corner. The north face is the veil between our enslaved conscious self and our freed collective conscious self. Every night when you fall asleep, your consciousness passes through the north face veil of the Tzolk'in Clock. Knowing where your consciousness goes every time you sleep answers the same question as to where we came from before being born and where we go after death. The Tzolk'in Clock shows the answer.

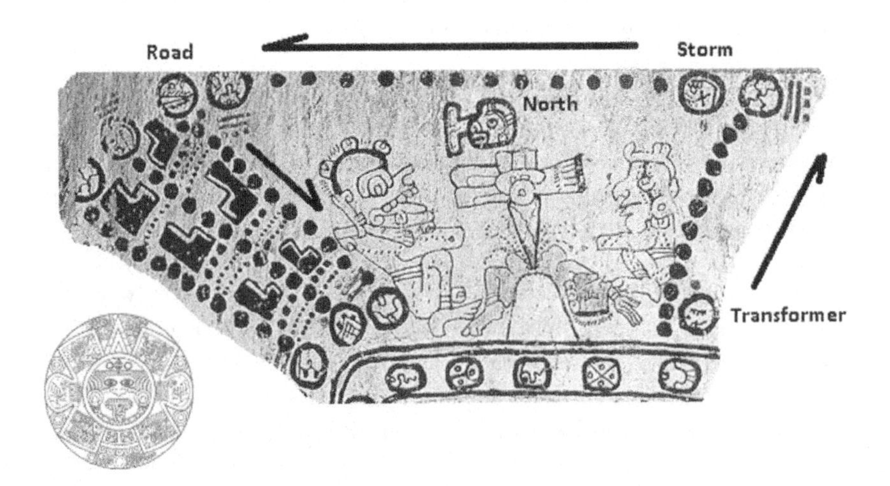

Many people would think this (see previous page) is an image of a painful sacrifice, just as we've been told the Aztec sun calendar is thirsty for human blood. However, the opposite is true for both. This image on the north face of the Tzolk'in Clock, as depicted in the Madrid codex, is showing yourself being released from your body, as you do every time you sleep and ultimately death. (Note: Birth is represented in this image to the discerning eye.) The Aztec sun calendar shows mother earth talking to you as you read this since, collectively, we are remembering her spiritual time. Mother earth is talking to us now. We are the people she is speaking to. This is the time to hear her words.

Our seeds are being grown in our collective consciousness during the north face of the Tzolk'in Clock. This is the time that your spiritual self helps create your physical self's reality. We are not alone in this realm; we are collectively working together. Yet, the definition of "we" in that sentence is different than the physical "we." Consider the spirits that make up your consciousness as individual as all the cells of your body going different places and then reuniting the moment you wake up. The north face of the Tzolk'in Clock represents the veil to this place.

This is where trust and faith come into play. Do you trust your spiritual self? Also, do trust that obstacles are presented to help you find your reality? Using the Tzolk'in Clock and trusting your spiritual self to bring your physical self reality is the key to creating your reality. Manifesting reality is just one aspect of this humanistic, spiritual timekeeper.

North Face Health Tip

Prepare for the upcoming Road trecena on the north face of the Tzolk'in Clock. Humans are designed to walk at least 10-15 minutes in a path every day, preferably on grass. This is important for your spiritual self to create your destiny. It gives momentum to the spiritual farming process. Walking gives a boost of energy to all the organs in your body with each step. It has the same effect on your spiritual energy and connects with mother earth's energy. This is free, natural energy available for your body, spirit and mind.

Tracking a Newborn's Time on the Tzolk'in

It's simple to count days with the Tzolk'in. For instance, you look forward to a baby's 260th day to celebrate their energy (and, first Tzolk'in birthday). Then, it's easy to track and congratulate them on 300 days, 400 days, etc. A child is 520 days old on their second Tzolk'in birthday, and you continue to remember to congratulate them for turning 600 days, etc. The sense of years becomes less important when every day becomes a birthday celebration. It’s also fun when people ask you a child’s age and you give it to them in days. Watch as they try to convert it!

Four Suits of Cards and Four Directions

It's interesting that a deck of cards is four suits of 13 each. This is equivalent to four trecenas. Perhaps each of the suits (clubs, spades, diamonds, and hearts) represents each of the four directions. It would be nice to play a deck showing Transformer, Monkey, Wisdom and Crocodile. But why stop there? Consider a new deck using all twenty trecenas. This deck would have 260 cards instead of just 52. Would that be considered "playing with a full deck?" Which suit would you pair with each of the cornerstones of the Tzolk'in Clock?

East Face Cornerstone	Crocodile	club spade heart diamond
North Face Cornerstone	Transformer	spade heart diamond club
West Face Cornerstone	Monkey	heart diamond club spade
South Face Cornerstone	Wisdom	diamond club spade heart

1-Transformer	Today begins the north face—a time to explore your other world; your spiritual world. The Maya knew this world very well and there was a thinner veil between it and their physical selves. Collectively, they could live in this realm, and perhaps still do.
2-Deer	After exploring the "other" world yesterday, today needs the strength and stability of a deer. These next few trecenas are all about the "other" world.
3-Star	You have companions in the spiritual realm. Share yourself with them as you sleep. Remember them when you wake up.
4-Water	This is the day that your physical self is immersed into the spiritual realm but is necessary for spiritual growth.
5-Dog	A dog follows your every move. He sleeps close to you and protects you. He loves going places with you and starts jumping and kissing you, when you put on shoes to go for a walk. That's the kind of energy of today. These next days, until 13-Storm, are the days to disconnect with your daily obligations. Take your dog energy with you. Hold his leash with your hand.
6-Monkey	A day to contemplate misconceptions in life. This is a good day to know what is going on truthfully and what is being deceptive. Trust your instincts.
7-Road	Walk with only those you trust today, especially in the spiritual realm.
8-Reed	Enhance what is important in your life, diminish what is not. Your seeds are turning into plants. Inspect them and help them grow.
9-Jaguar	The fertile power of physical energy is strong today. You get a good sense of which plants are growing, and you feel strength from knowing.
10-Eagle	Let negativity dissolve. Wash your hands of it.
11-Wisdom	Meditate about your physical reality, in the calm placid waters of your spiritual being. Give guidance to the fertile fields growing.

12-Earthquake	Center your heart as your spiritual self creates your future reality.
13-Flint	A mental and heartfelt image of your new self is formed as the fruit of this trecena. Relax and enjoy your bountiful produce that will soon be reality.

STORM

The Storm (Rainstorm) trecena is prominently located on the north face of the Tzolk'in Clock. This trecena is deeply connected to our sleep selves—the place we go when we are asleep. Spend time with meditation. Keep calm and placid waters in your mind and heart. Your sleep self is taking care of your future reality during this trecena.

The Madrid codex north face looks gruesome below. It represents transformation from awake to sleep each night and ultimately death.

Depicted is an obsidian knife releasing energy from a human body, which is laying on rock, we notice a big 'X" shown on the knife. There seems to be a spirit flying over the obsidian knife, holding it from its heart and overlooking the process. The Olmec, Aztec and Maya lived on this spiritual calendar. The Gregorian calendar captures your time and deflects your spiritual sense of time.

Waking up in the morning on the Gregorian calendar, do you ask yourself: *What day is it?*, *What time is it?*, and *How much free time do I have before getting ready?* In contrast, waking up on the Tzolk'in calendar, you ask yourself: *What is today's energy?*, *How am I feeling in relation to what I know about the day's energy?*, and *What's the best way to handle today?*

The Gregorian calendar way of living opposes the natural experience of the Tzolk'in Clock and especially this trecena. Separate yourself from it because this trecena is like being in the jungle, in the rain, naked and on rocks with water rushing by to feed plants and animals. There are no 9AM meetings scheduled for the north side of the Tzolk'in Clock. Save that energy for the south side of the Tzolk'in Clock (the opposite trecena is the Water trecena). That trecena is the time to take physical action to fulfill your destiny.

Sitting inside of the Tzolk'in Clock, facing east and with the walls folded upwards, you can see there are outlooks that directly face each other. Could there be special connections between two outlooks? As you can see the 13-Crocodile outlook is directly opposite of the 1-Storm outlook, just as 1-Water is opposite of 13-Monkey. If there is a special relationship, it could be a "soulmate," or the lack of narcissism in a relationship, or even mind reading. Does the Tzolk'in Clock hold special patterns? Does 1 connect to 13 as shown, or does 1 connect to 12? If 1 connects to 12, then it explains the feeling of people born on the thirteenth day of a trecena, since they

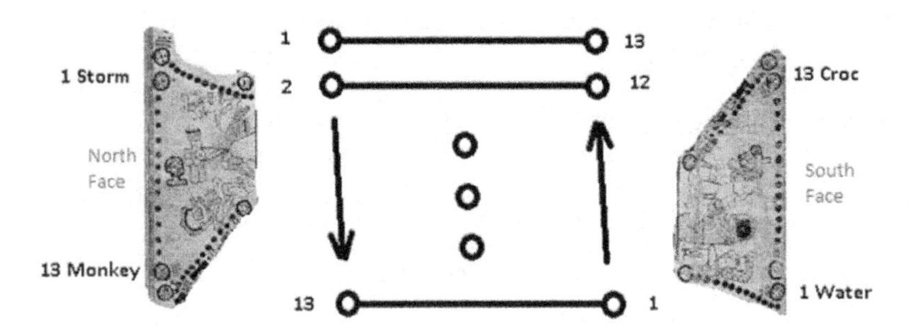

would not have a soulmate connect with anyone, but yet connected with all other 13th day people. I believe the later is true.

It would be good to have a retreat with 260 different people, each with one of the outlooks. We could have activities that may or may not unlock some of these special patterns. For instance, would four people from each side of the Tzolk'in Clock, collectively, have a better view on an issue than four people from the same side of the Tzolk'in Clock? Perhaps, individually, we lack the capstone of our consciousness and collectively we can gain complete understanding. We all have God–like power within us, but it has been capped off. Imagine collectively unlocking the full power of the Tzolk'in Clock.

The Rainstorm trecena is the deepest spiritual trecena. It's equivalent to traveling through the right brain of consciousness. Dr. Jill Taylor explains the right brain of consciousness in her book, *A Stroke of Insight.* She describes the right brain (north face of the Tzolk'in Clock) as euphoria of the intuitive and a sense of complete well–being and peace. Comparing the Tzolk'in Clock to a human brain, the rainstorm trecena is deep in the right brain. This trecena is a time for meditation. Put pure ingredients into your body. It is a good time for fasting, purification and staying away from poisonous items like alcohol.

The Gregorian calendar way of living gives you self-created life. The Tzolk'in Clock way of living gives you our creator's power. The north face, and especially this trecena, is the time to let your spiritual self take care of the plants growing in your heart, soul and mind. Keep the materialistic way of living to a minimum so it doesn't interfere with your natural way of creating. The north face of the Tzolk'in Clock is the time to envision your future self, life, and surroundings. The seeds you planted on the east face are being farmed out by your sleep consciousness. Physically, there is not much that can be done. The growth happens naturally. Your best effort now is positive meditation and peace in your heart. Good things take a lot of work. Great things happen all at once. This trecena is about letting those great things manifest in our spiritual selves so they can be created in our physical reality.

1-Rainstorm	Imagine the most perfect place on earth. This trecena is about being in that place both physically and spiritually. This Rainstorm trecena is like being in the jungle with fresh water on stones next to plants and their shade from the sun.
2-Light	Associate with our Indian and Shaman ancestral past. This video may help: https://youtu.be/lFuGwkwfm2k
3-Crocodile	What a difference a day makes! The duality of yesterday has cracked open and a new intention is emerging. It's a good feeling.
4-Wind	Be aware that you are aware. Soak in all the senses without fear of the future, nor regrets of the past, and loving the moment, continuously. Hold water that is clear, placid and calm. Experience nature and watch the stars in the sky.
5-House	Today will strengthen your heart as this energy gives a constructive healing energy to your Akbal, or house, or internal flame.
6-Seed	Separate yourself from the materialistic life. Try to ignore the Gregorian calendar and your physical desires. Stay calm.
7-Serpent	Meditate on the water in your body. Take some water and pray into it. Open the magic in your heart and fill the water with light.
8-Transformer	Today is the "Day of the Dead". It's the day of the place you go to every time you fall asleep. Its energy connects with your ancestors.
9-Deer	The energy of this trecena is moving like tropical storm. Today's Deer energy gives your strength and a solid foundation. The Deer energy offers loving thoughts, loving words, loving inflections, loving actions. It revives your heart.
10-Star	Today you are able to step out, mentally, and appreciate life. It's not about the pot of gold at the end of the rainbow, just enjoy the rainbow.
11-Water	Today's energy is natural. Appreciate the art of humans and the majesty of nature. We are deep into this trecena and the heart of natural existence.

12-Dog	As the trecena ends, the reality of the Gregorian calendar is a heavy burden. Collectively, we can be stronger without materialistic worries.
13-Monkey	This is the energy of a sunset on the ocean, when the sun makes the shape of a cross in the sky and water and reflection. Enjoy today's energy. Tomorrow is 1-Road; the *Ye shall know the truth and the truth shall make you free* energy.

ROAD

A trecena starts with the first day's intention at the base (1-Road) and targets its last day's intention (13-Seed). Our seeds planted on the east face and currently on the north face of the Tzolk'in Clock have just gone through the Rainstorm trecena deep within our sleep consciousness. Now, the seeds must travel the Road trecena to be presented to our collective consciousness for judgment. Travel on the Road trecena with honesty, trust and responsibility. Envision and prepare your new self for the west face of the Tzolk'in Clock, where your seeds will be judged by our collective consciousness.

The Road trecena is about appreciating what you already have without falling off balance to create your future reality. Balance your current self reality with the growth of your new reality. Living in the moment is the best way to have balance. Let the confidence of your future reality give you strength to do what you want in the present. Your vision of your future self is coming.

The north face of the Tzolk'in Clock, as shown in the Fejervary codex, consists of the Transformer (Death) trecena, the Rain (Rainstorm) trecena and the Road (Grass) trecena. The northwest corner of the Tzolk'in Clock consists of the Serpent (Snake) trecena and the Flint trecena.

6 Miquiztli (Death) 7 Quiáhuitl (Rain) 8 Malinalli (Grass) 9 Cóatl (Snake) 10 Técpatl (Flint)

This trecena is a collective test and personal challenge. Can you bare the change of your new intentions? The strength of your growth will be tested this trecena. The seeds planted begin another stage of development through the northwest corner of the Tzolk'in Clock (the Serpent and Flint trecenas). This Road trecena takes us towards our collective consciousness. Our seeds will get a fresh burst of cleansing on 8-Storm. Your sleep self has worked on your intentions this past Storm trecena. This trecena brings your future self into the present for our collective conscious to review during the west face of the Tzolk'in Clock.

Here, the Fejervary Codex shows the North and Northwest sides of the Tzolk'in:

It is important to take a moment and see where we are on the Tzolk'in Clock viewed in 3D, with each of the eight walls folded upright. You are sitting in the center of the Tzolk'in Clock looking east. Since 1-Crocodile, time has passed from the front (east) to the left (northeast) and around (north). The Road trecena is the last one of the north face. Use the Aztec version of the Tzolk'in to visualize traveling the Road trecena before starting the Serpent trecena. The Serpent is shown as the animal face with fangs.

Each dot on the Tzolk'in Clock is a unique outlook on life. You get your birth outlook for 52 years and then you get a second outlook. This gives elder perspective. The Tzolk'in, viewed in 3D, is a way to see from where each person gets their unique point of view. This way of viewing your interactions with other people lets you know the foundation of their way of seeing things. This enhances communication and builds trust in the community living on the spiritual way of knowing time. Our materialistic life, living with the Gregorian calendar, is almost completely at odds with the Tzolk'in Clock. Gregorian calendar people become machine-like and less human without realizing it. It's like they can't put their finger on what's wrong and are greatly distracted with their nine-to-five obligations.

Here's an example of spiritual time. In September 2011, I traveled to Centre Lothlorien in France to a Peace Festival for my first experience with Maya Guatemala Grandmothers Elisabeth Aurojo and Nana Vilma and Maya Colombians Paco and Nasly Quiroga. The schedule said they would do their morning ceremony at 9AM. Events were scheduled by the hour, but they were nowhere to be found. As nearly 100 of us waited in a large circle, they arrived from the nearby river. The translator said that their concept of time is different than ours. It sent a ripple through the obligatory schedule that has resonated with me since. However, sometimes the Gregorian calendar can be useful for manifesting your reality, especially around the south face and the Water trecena.

The Road trecena leads us back to our awake selves, but we are still in the Transformer side. We take our seeds planted on the east side and carry them through the north side and give them to the west side, where our collective conscious will judge the worthiness of our new intentions. You should use the Tzolk'in spiritual time and journal for a year or two to see the difference. Writing you thoughts on, for instance, March 3rd doesn't give any useful spiritual meaning to your day. Comparatively, entering thoughts on, for instance, a 7-Serpent day will resonate your thoughts with the day's natural energy. A good way to set your day's intentions is to pray to the east before the rays of the sun touch your body. This is a Navajo way, too!

1-Road	The Christian cross looks like the sun setting on a water horizon with its light reflected across the water towards your feet. This is the road that lets you walk on water. To keep your path clear, meditate on calm and placid water. Balance your present moment with your future self.
2-Reed	We are part of a larger collective consciousness. We can only do our part for the whole. Everything is as it should be. Enjoy each moment.
3-Jaguar	Three is a day to think about family with emergence of animal instincts from the wilderness. Be ready to jump into a 4-Eagle day.
4-Eagle	A good day to see things from high with the stability of the four directions. Bless your calm, placid and clear water with loving thoughts and with the readiness to accept new intentions.
5-Wisdom	Appreciate your personal freedoms and your community connections. This is a day of happiness.
6-Earth	If you were not afraid, who would you be? Release anything holding you back.
7-Flint	Feel your sleep self's work to the new you being created. Enjoy the new you.
8-Storm	In classical Maya civilization (before the dark ages), children would learn about their sleep Nawals. When you get to know your Nawal, as a real entity in your life, it can be very beneficial. Your Nawals help create your reality for you.
9-Sun	Your sleep Nawal and friends are having their goodbye celebration as your new self is ready for presentation.
10-Crocodile	The eyes see above, while the body floats below. What will you see today?
11-Wind	A test run of your new self. Enjoy.
12-House	Today is a deep resonance with your home, especially that time when you first awake. It's that moment of remembering your dreams, before focusing on the present.

13-Seed	Today is a natural Sunday on the 13-day (seven days and six nights) trecena. Reap your fruit from the past week's energy and plan for your next trecena. Your new self will ebb and flow through the next trecena with spectacular results.

SERPENT & FLINT (PART I)

This article is about both the Serpent and Flint trecenas, with a focus on the Serpent trecena. Part two will focus on the Flint trecena. It is important to see how the two trecenas of a corner work. The Tzolk'in Clock has four faces and four corners. The faces on the Tzolk'in as depicted in the Madrid codex have the words east, north, west and south written in the Maya language. Each face has three trecenas and each corner has two trecenas. Corner trecenas work together to release the energy of each direction into our collective consciousness. The Tzolk'in "birthday wishes" of all people born on the north face are offered to our collective consciousness on these next two trecenas. People born on faces are the coaches of the team and people born on corners are the players of the team, with each team being east, north, west or south. If the Tzolk'in is fixed, then the faces are the mast and the corners are the sails of each direction. It's interesting that people born on corners tend to stir things up. It's also interesting that "teammates" born on a face and a corner will be good friends. One gives stability and the other gives dynamics, and they are both on the same team (east, north, west or south).

The Tzolk'in is the driving calendar for all other calendars (sun, moon, and stars). Corner trecenas give spin to all calendars. This is how it interacts. The face trecenas give strength. The corner trecenas give motion. Corner trecenas are the teeth in a drill bit that create space and time. Without this rotation, there would be no life. However, if the Tzolk'in is fixed, then it gives rotation as time passes through it. The only physical connection of the Tzolk'in Clock to time on earth is the sun, as each day is a new energy.

Here, we see the northwest corner of the Tzolk'in from the Fejervary and Madrid codices:

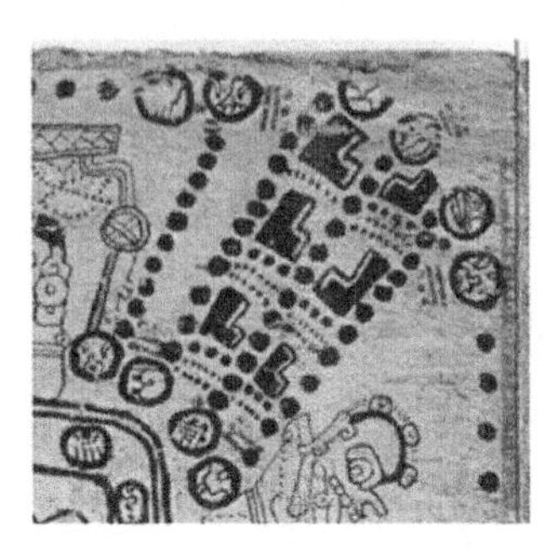

The start of the Serpent trecena is shown in the Fejervary codex as a snake's head with 2 fangs.

The start of the Flint trecena is shown inside of a parrot. The tree between the northwest trecenas has transformed from the tree in the northeast corner, and now has tripod roots with a vine and four berries. The hummingbird (south) has risen from the northeast corner. This is symbolic of our seeds being passed around the Tzolk'in.

The Madrid codex shows both the first day and the last day of the trecena, emphasizing the direction of travel from the first day towards the last day.

This trecena goes from Serpent to Earth (Earthquake). The next trecena goes from Flint to Dog. If you count the number of dots on the Madrid codex Tzolk'in from Serpent to Earth, there are 14 dots, not 13. This has

been attributed to haste of the artist and occurs at other places on the Madrid codex depiction of the Tzolk'in.

It's been noted, by Merideth Paxton in her book, *The Cosmos of the Yucatec Maya, Cycles and Steps from the Madrid Codex*, that the footsteps (L-shapes) represent the months of the Ha'ab and the little dots represent the days of the Ha'ab. These shapes and dots are omitted on the faces of the Tzolk'in Clock. Each dot of the Ha'ab is not a fixed date. Instead, they revolve around the Tzolk'in and repeat the cycle every 52 Ha'ab years. This directly connects the Tzolk'in Clock to the solar year calendar and the location of the stars above us. The Tzolk'in Clock is the interaction of all these aspects of the Tzolk'in.

The Tzolk'in Clock should be viewed like sitting in a hoogan with its furnace in the center (shown as a flame in the Madrid codex). There is a small opening in the top of the hoogan to see the moon and stars at night. The Jaguar trecena of the east face walks over the door of the Tzolk'in Clock. We just completed the north face to our left and are beginning the northwest corner of the hoogan. Imagine yourself sitting at the center and your internal flame is the furnace. As the days pass, the dot representing the day on the Tzolk'in Clock lights up as the previous day dims. This cycle repeats every 260 days.

In our hoogan version of the Tzolk'in Clock, each of the Ha'ab dots light up. We can follow the Ha'ab through the Tzolk'in. Merideth Paxton identified the top 5.25 dots between the 13-Deer and 1-Star on the southeast corner of the Tzolk'in Clock as the 5.25 Wajeb days. The days of the Ha'ab are for this Serpent trecena (March 2019) will light up in the east to north corner of the hoogan (left most picture on opposite page). The Wajeb occurred on February 15-20, 2019. That means the Ha'ab is in the northeast corner (bottom six dots of right most picture on opposite page), while the Tzolk'in is in the northwest corner during this round through the Serpent and Flint trecenas. This is the current energy of time and space while living on Tzolk'in time. This all would be better represented inside of a hoogan with lights on the walls to match the Tzolk'in and Ha'ab time. At night, the moon shadow would also interact via the small opening in the top. It is similar to how the Tzolk'in and Ha'ab interact at the Temple of Kukulcan in Chichen Itza on the Spring and Fall equinoxes of each year, repeating the pattern every 52 Ha'ab years.

1-Serpent	A seed planted will spout and grow using God's energy. A trecena works the same way. Plant the seed today, and over the next 13 days, it gives fruition. Unlike a wish, there is a method to developing its reality. It's like putting a wish inside of a seed and planting that seed in the fertile soil of your mind, body and spirit. It's like there's a garden in your mind. You pull weeds and plant new seeds in your Akbal (House). The Tzolk'in Clock seeds take all 20 trecenas to bare fruition.
2-Transformer	Today represents duality and transformation (birth, sleep or death) and also remembers our ancestors. This is a challenging day to be born as there is a strong connection to our ancestors. In today's materialistic time, it must be especially difficult.
3-Deer	Today should be an excellent day for parents, with the energy of 3 being a family day to spend with your germinated seeds. Take today off—no work, no practice, just relaxation.
4-Star	Do you ever feel surrounded by annoyance? Do you feel that something is not right, like being in a heavenly place pervaded with wickedness? Prey for the reunification of the four directions today.
5-Water	Water days are days to offer yourself to others. It's also a day to pay bills. So should I pay today or wait another 20 days? Water days are good for "row, row, row your boat." Just go with the flow and admire the journey. The Tzolk'in gives you a spiritual view of each day.
6-Dog	The sun is setting and the energy of 5-Water is waning. The energy of 6-Dog is rising. When I was in Belize, I got to play with a water dog. A water dog is an otter that has a personality of a dog. Dog days are known for rock and roll. It's an especially good day for everyone born on the 6th inflection of any day.

7-Monkey	Today is a very playful day. Playful opportunities present themselves to help you choose your next path, or road, or destiny. This happens every 20 days, but 7 days are most powerful. As a metaphor, consider the Wizard of Oz. Today is the day to pick your yellow brick road. Tomorrow is the day to walk down the road you picked. 9-Reed is the day to meet the Wizard and have a conversation. This is all part of the Serpent energy that gives us many ups and downs.
8-Road	The sun, moon, stars and rainbows are your guide. With your feet on the ground and the sky above, you are the movement of time and space. You are the butterfly.
9-Reed	Reconnect the 4 directions with loving thoughts, words and intentions. Together we can collectively be a part of our moral consciousness. Let everyone on earth hear you today.
10-Jaguar	Today is a day to pounce and catch your prey, but you must be prepared. Sometimes it's better not to pounce. Perhaps it's better to use your big Jaguar paws and lick your kittens.
11-Eagle	Today is an active and loving day in which dreams come true. Enjoy.
12-Widsom	Today is day to feel the threads of your spider web. Be still, calm, and contemplate. It can be humbling and uplifting.
13-Earthquake	The transition from last night to today can feel extremely depressing as you are deeply immersed into the Serpent energy. Yesterday was spent deep within. Expect the opposite to happen today as you emerge back above water. The Serpent trecena has exaggerated waves of 7 days and 6 nights. Tomorrow starts the Flint trecena. This will be the time for deep introspection and cleansing, so spend today enjoying the seeds that have borne fruit this trecena.

SERPENT & FLINT (PART II)

The Tzolk'in Clock relates daily energy to our minds, hearts and spirits and is a human connection with divinity. It is also a Clock to create your reality and its three dimensional representation locates your outlook and the outlook of others. It's deeply rooted to your chakras and describes both our awake and asleep consciousness. These articles are a look at this ancient understanding of time.

We flew with the Eagle three days ago, gained wisdom two days ago, and plunged inside of ourselves for deep introspection yesterday. The flexible serpent trecena is over and we now begin the firming Flint trecena. Your new reality is cast into stone this trecena. It will be presented to our collective consciousness during the monkey, seed and earth trecenas. Let your connection with flint consciousness do the work for you. Shape your future self while the stone is soft. Let the magic of life transform you.

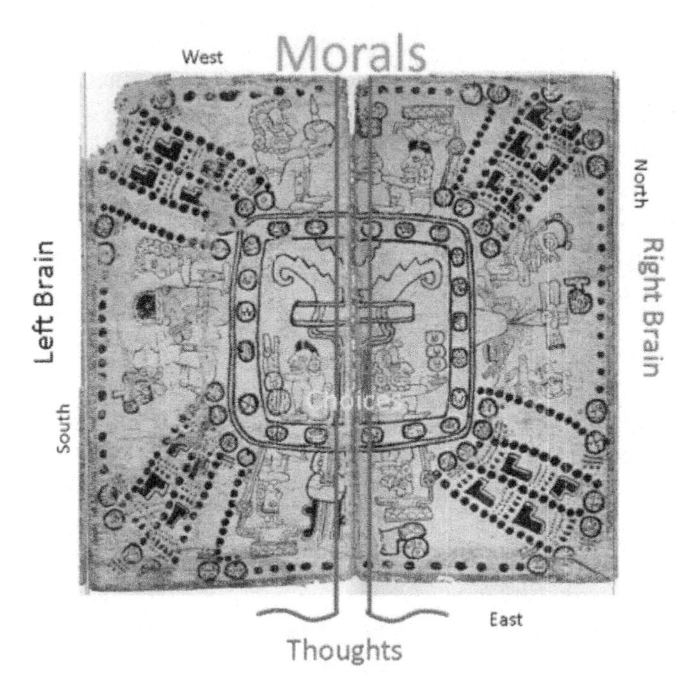

The Serpent and Flint trecenas are located in the corner between the north face and west face of the Tzolk'in Clock (top right). People born on flint days make excellent mirrors for other people. They help you see yourself. They help you cut out negativity in your Akbal. The Serpent trecena was wavy. The Flint trecena solidifies, as we transition from north to west. Sitting in your internal Akbal in the hoogan analogy, facing east, the northwest trecena is located at your back left, in the corner. It's located between your left side and the back of your head on the mind analogy.

The seeds you planted on the Crocodile trecena have passed through the east face, east to north corner, and the north face. We are, now, in the northwest corner. The seeds are about to be presented to the west face, starting with the Monkey trecena. The west face is about morals, choosing right or wrong (and the associated guilt), and is always changing with our collective consciousness. As we pass through the west face, starting with 1-Monkey, our seeds will update our collective morals. Our seeds will also transition from the right brain to the left brain on 8-Monkey. This Flint trecena is about polishing our seeds (the final details) before being presented to the west face of the Tzolk'in Clock.

The Flint trecena gives you tools and mirrors to clean your Akbal and remove any guilt. The best way to keep your Akbal clean is to not create guilt. Use guilt as a rudder to steer your choices. If a choice makes you feel guilty then reject or ignore it. Guilt can also build up on the west face of the Tzolk'in Clock and have a spiraling effect to make choosing right from wrong harder to see. The Flint trecena is a good time to scrape any guilt that has accumulated on your morals. Finally, once it's been scraped, cleaned and polished, be sure to sweep clean the sandy floor of your hoogan/Akbal. An analogy would be to clean your oven in your kitchen. The Akbal is the energy or flame that passes through you. Once the Flint trecena has ended, enjoy the freshness of your mind, heart and spirit. This trecena is a good time to update your kitchen, bedroom or whichever part you want the flame to burn brighter for the next Tzolk'in round.

The cutting tool of flint has consciousness. Think of an obsidian knife and how long the consciousness has existed in it and how long you exist compared to it. Synchronizing your resonance with the Flint trecena will make cleaning and polishing more effective. There are some areas that need the Flint harshness to be cleaned. This is the trecena to do that. What hardened areas are there in your Akbal that will help you when removed? Maya pyramids are evidence of our ability to connect with stone. Use the strength of the Flint trecena to create yourself. Grow your stone temples this trecena as a foundation for the Tzolk'in round. Empower your seeds to endure the test of time. Flint people can also be like cement in a group of people. They are the connective tissue of the collective energy and help with cohesiveness in a group.

Maya birthdays are days of intense resonance with the day's energy. Maya trecenas are similar, but on a slower vibration. You have a slight "breeze to your back" on your trecena. If you were born on a 1-Flint, 2-Flint, etc. then this trecena will have a pleasant vibration with your natural energy. If you became an elder on a flint day, this trecena will give you an uplifting vibration.

Trecenas are an excellent way to manifest short term wishes or goals. You can plan an activity to begin on 1-Flint and use the ebb and flow of the 7 days and 6 nights to manifest your reality. You can do this physically or spiritually, such as clean your house or cleaning your internal house (Akbal). There are many ways to clean your Akbal. Thoughts enter your Akbal from the east, then you choose to accept, reject or ignore using the morals on the west. If you go against your morals then guilt can spill out into your Akbal similar to getting your oven dirty, or the floors of a hoogan dirty. It's always good to keep your Akbal clean. Using the energy of the Flint trecena gives you extra ability, similar to a steel wool brush for cleaning. This is important before we enter the west face of collective judgment.

Everyone feels a change in each day's energy. Each day has a unique resonance that matches or conflicts with your internal flame.

1-Flint	Plan for this trecena today. Get all the tools you need (physically and spiritually). This is the trecena to cleanse your mind, heart and soul. Clear out space for new thoughts, emotions, and spirit.
2-Storm	This is a soft energy. From Jagaur Wisdom: Kawoq can be a highly emotional day, a quality which has the potential to either entangle us in a storm of uncontrolled feelings or to bring us in touch with the deep spiritual resources of the heart. On a 2 day, interpersonal relationships are the path which leads to those deep recesses of the heart. Care for those you love. Don't be afraid to let your real feeling shine forth.
3-Light	Good visibility. The third inflection typically means family, as it takes 3 people to make a family. It might be a painful day, as we see clearer today, for self-healing. You will be seeing all of your mistakes that have been buried in your consciousness. Let the pain go, like a snake shedding its skin.
4-Crocodile	Internal cracking. This is the day of 4, stable like legs of an animal, immersed in sacred water, with light entering its eyes from above the water's surface. It's that moment you walk out of water, or emerge from the womb. It's a birthing of ideas and spiritual growth. It's also a night time energy (2, 4, 6, 8, 10 and 12), which is a rest day. Let the water energy carry you down the stream.
5-Wind	Today is the best day for powerful communications, such as a protest, political speech, etc. It can also result in saying the something that shouldn't have been said, since it's so tempting to speak your mind today. Be empathetic to others, thinking about what they are going through.

6-House	Today's energy is represented by the first change from night to day. Sitting in the hoogan, with the door open, you could notice how heavenly this change happens. It's the idea that each day is your most valuable gift—a blessing. It's also the third night of the trecena, which is made of 7 days and 6 nights. Since it's a nighttime energy, let the energy move you, rather than activity move in it. Let blessings come to you today. Tomorrow you can actively manifest, or package these blessings into seeds to plant for fruition. The Gregorian calendar doesn't explain this, but the Tzolk'in calendar does.
7-Seed	Feel the benefit. If you could do anything or have anything, what would it be and why? Our blessing is to realize mortality and cherish every moment.
8-Serpent	Today's energy is like your internal energy wave that flows up your chakras and sheds your skin for tomorrow. Today can be a day of ups and downs, so minimize your loses and maximize your gains, like trading on the market. There is a tail whip from our previous Serpent trecena.
9-Transformer	Leave your mark in the soft stone. Let it harden. Death is just one name, it could also be birth, or transformation from sleep to wake and back again. It also involves our ancestors and connecting with their life.
10-Deer	Proudly walk the earth. After yesterday's most significant day for self healing, today, we get the stability and morality of the Deer, on the tenth day of this Flint trecena. Many people associate 10 days, as the application of your 10 fingers to get something done.
11-Star 	Accept your destiny. There are several references to this day. The Maya word translates to star or Venus. The Aztec translates to rabbit. Different dialects say Q'anil and Lamat. It is more like the ripening of corn. The dots in this symbol are the morning star and evening star, Venus, as it rises into the morning sky and descends and then rises in the evening sky and then descends.

12-Water	Here we go! The new reality you wanted. Water days are good for paying your debt and appreciating reciprocity. It's especially important, as we end the 65 days of transformation. Today is the day to wash it all off. Tomorrow will be a day of dancing with our ancestors and remembering who we are and why we are here. Gather some natural spring water. Bathe under a waterfall. Cleanse your spirit today.
13-Dog	Celebrate and give thanks to your spiritual self. Today is the day of cosmic friendship. We have just been submerged in 65 days of transformation, ending on the Flint trecena, and we are about to begin the next 65 days focusing on morals. Before we do that, we need to celebrate all that we have learned these past 65 days.

MONKEY

In the image below, we see a depiction of your awake self offering a seed (goal/intention) to your Nawal (or, sleep self) who is connected to our collective consciousness. This is the seed you conceived on the east face. Your seeds will be judged by our collective consciousness along the west face. Our collective consciousness will also be updated as we travel along the west face. 1-Monkey is the first day on the west face of the Tzolk'in Clock (bottom right circle) and ends on 13-House (top right circle). The west face (Monkey, Seed and Earth trecenas) is about our collective morals and right versus wrong. This is the time when our seeds get judged and appreciated. It's also a time when our collective consciousness gets updated. We transition from right to left on 8-Monkey (top center dot).

Today we begin to immerse ourselves into the collective consciousness. People born on the west side are good at seeing all sides of things. They make good arbitrators and help with social decisions. Our morals are based on our collective consciousness, knowing right from wrong, based on what we collectively believe. You might say the east side is the pitcher of thoughts and the west side is the catcher. We steer the ball along the way. Sometimes people have trouble making decisions, and people on the west (the catchers) are good at helping us make decisions by giving advice and leadership. Imagine you are in a hoogan and the west face is on the wall behind you. As you face east, thoughts enter your mind in front, you chose to accept, reject or ignore them based on the morals on the back (west face). People born on the west face are good managers of others, as they tend to be fair.

This time of life is interesting since the internet is allowing our awake consciousness to connect across earth. Although it's still limited since few different languages are connecting, the English language is thoroughly connected. Morals are being spread over the internet and connecting with different cultures as we are awake. The same happens as we sleep. Our consciousness connects with the collective consciousness. During the west face, the seeds of your future reality are presented to the collective consciousness as an update to you and to also update our collective consciousness.

The analogy of the hoogan with the central furnace to your Akbal is fitting. The monkey trecena ends on 13-House/Akbal. Imagine the west face of the hoogan as the collective consciousness connected to your mind as you make choices, deciding what is right and what is wrong. You sit in the center of your hoogan/Akbal as thoughts stream in through the front door on the east face. If you choose to do something that makes you feel guilty, it's based on the morals of our collective consciousness on the west face. The space between you and the west face of the hoogan/Akbal, should be the cleanest. This is your personal connection with life. You can help others keep their area clean as well. Many people ask you for advice. Your answer should be based on if it makes them keep that area clean or if it creates dirt. Guilt creates dirt in the area behind you and your west face. The west face of the Tzolk'in Clock is the current status of all living consciousness. Each time we pass through the west face, our collective consciousness is updated. Our understanding of right and wrong is different since the time of our great, great grandparents, and it will be different for our great, great grandchildren.

Knowing everyone's Tzolk'in birthday helps our social interactions. Collectively we become aware of our strengths and weaknesses.

Knowing someone born on your Tzolk'in birthday is helpful, as it helps us to see their similarities. You have 260 unique interactions with all others. And all others have their unique 260 interactions. Therefore your interaction with a person born on 6-Star, for example, will be a unique (1 in 260) interaction. Anyone born on a different day than you will get a different perspective of the same person born on 6-Star.

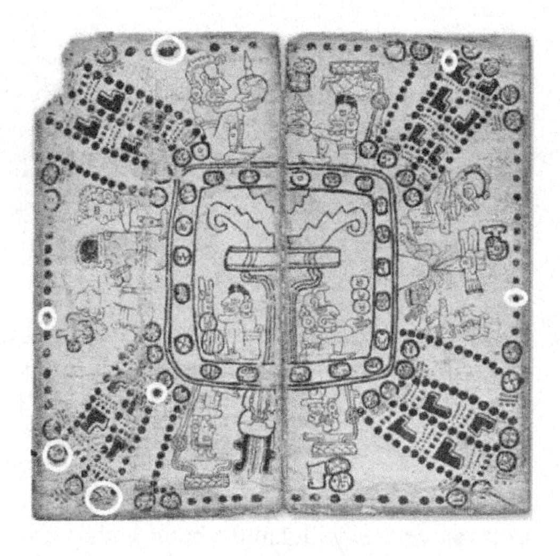

By mapping people who are in your circle of friends, you can see how they interact with you and with each other. Taking the people born (circled in white) you can better understand their interactions. It starts to make sense when people on the same direction seem to get along better. When two people face towards each other (imagine this image in 3D with the walls and corners folded upright) they can almost read each other's minds. People born on the same trecena feel like brothers and sisters. There is a coach/ player relationship with people born on the face and corner of the same direction. People born on faces are less likely to "stir things up" than people born on corners.

1-Monkey	The energy of 13-Dog is waning and the energy of 1-Monkey is building. It's the end of the past five north trecenas and the beginning of the next five west trecenas. The burden of time is being lifted off the shoulders of people born in the north and being placed on people born in the west. Feel mother earth and trust she will provide for you. The transformation is complete.
2-Road	Today is a day of duality. You might find yourself exploring new horizons or fighting with your family. Enjoy the destiny you are given. If it's tough, it will get better. It happens for a reason.
3-Reed	Today is the connection between man and God, especially as it's associated with family, home and body. See if you and two other people make a group today. Stir it up with your family today.
4-Jaguar	This day gives strength to our collective consciousness. This energy was absorbed on the Jaguar trecena and is the brace of the west face. It's always a lovely day to experience.
5-Eagle	Today's energy is lifting. It's a fun day to explore and to be a guide. It's about common courtesy and human decency. Connect your feet with earth as your mind and heart sail in the sky. Today will help you see the big picture and what decisions to make for a better life for everyone.
6-Wisdom	As the 4-Jaguar day gave support from the inside, 6-Wisdom gives support from our ancestors and future generations. This is a day of collective wisdom when truths can be shared. Today, we use our collective consciousness to decide what is right and wrong for all of us. Pay attention to your dreams, as you may get a glimpse of collective conscious activity.
7-Earthquake	Feel the energy today. It's a good day to cut loose ends or make decisions on which loose ends to cut. Today is the day to break out of conformity. Tomorrow is the day of introspection. And two days later is Rainstorm, to cleanse your heart, mind and soul.

8-Flint	Smile at people today and cut unhappiness out of your spirit. Connect with the community to heal your Akbal. If your surroundings are not benefiting you, it's a good time to express that to others.
9-Storm	We live in a created world. Plant a seed in soil with sunlight and water, and it grows. It makes fruit and other seeds. This is a creation. We are living in an organic realm. Our purpose is larger than our conscious experience. Think of where you go when you sleep. Think of how you transform when you wake up. You are enslaved in your mind and body, limited to a few senses. Yet, when you sleep, you experience our realm beyond our senses. Our sleeping selves have counter parts, called Nawals.
10-Ahau	There's a sense of relief on Ahau days. This 10-Ahau seems even better.
11-Crocodile	These past few days have a special purpose for the west side. It's been the setting of the foundation of our collective consciousness. Pray for the reunification of the four directions today.
12-Wind	Today is a day of deep meditation, to connect with your inner voice. This is the sixth night of the trecena, and it goes deeper than any other night. Using the connectivity of the monkey trecena on the day of god's breath is our deepest moment to experience oneness with God.
13-House	We are completing the first trecena of the west side. The cross from 7-Dog to 8-Monkey is a big deal to the Maya of Guatemala.

SEED

"Humankind has not woven the web of life. We are but one thread within it. Whatever we do to the web, we do to ourselves. All things are bound together. All things connect."

— Chief Seattle

The seed trecena connects us to our collective consciousness. Take any social issue and, as we pass through the seed trecena, we will update our collective consciousness. It will occur to others that something needs to be done to fix the issue. Today's issues are different than our parents' and grandparents' issues. Our collective consciousness is continually updated. The seed trecena is the time of this update and 8-Monkey is the day to celebrate it.

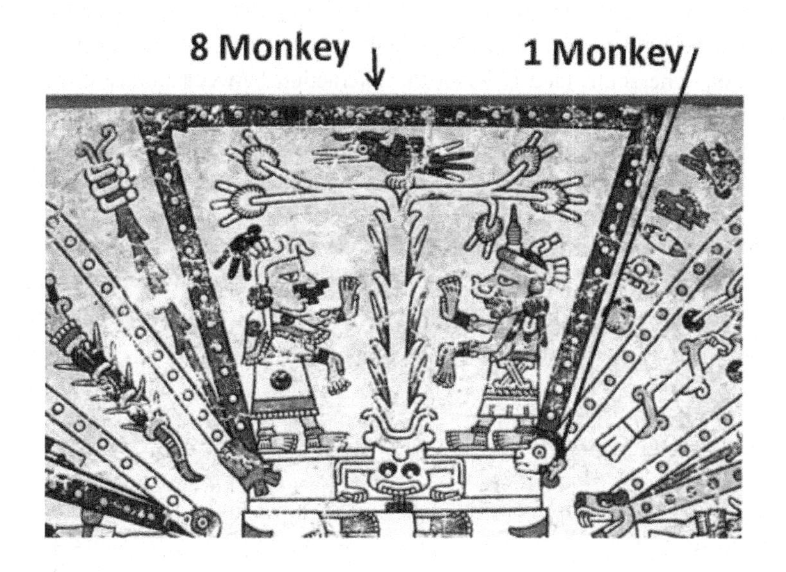

The picture above shows the west face of the Codex Fejervary-Mayer Tzolk'in. The setting moon has a maize plant gaining energy from it and a hummingbird (west) on top. The west face consists of the Monkey, Seed and Earth trecenas. The Seed trecena travels across the top, from left to right, with 8-Monkey along the way. The Seed trecena is deeply connected with our collective consciousness. It is the time our seeds of intention are judged for creation and the time that we update our collective consciousness.

Our seeds planted on the east face of the Tzolk'in Clock (about 130 days ago) have passed through the east face, the east-north corner, the north face, the northwest corner and now passes across the west face. The west face, and especially the seed trecena, interacts with our collective consciousness, our morals, our knowing right from wrong and making choices. You are gaining a new perspective on your future self. It now seems possible to have everything you requested on the east face of the Tzolk'in Clock. Ideas are flowing how to make it happen. Ideas of what you need to physically do are coming to you.

You are less connected to your seeds this trecena as they are being judged, but you will be re-empowered, especially beginning the south face at the start the Wisdom trecena. The Seed trecena ends on 13-Wisdom. Carry the wisdom you learn this trecena and apply it during the Wisdom trecena at the beginning of the south face, when it is time to take action to have your fruition. The south face is when the interaction between the Tzolk'in and Ha'ab, or Gregorian calendar, mostly occurs. The south face is the time to gather the fruits of fruition from your seeds planted on the east face of the Tzolk'in Clock.

8-Monkey happens as our consciousness passes the midline of the Tzolk'in Clock. This day is shown on the Tzolk'in Fejervary and Madrid codices crossing from right to left at the mid-plane. This relates to our corpus callosum and going from the right brain into the left brain. Here, time changes from passive to active.

The Tzolk'in Mind

The Tzolk'in is a three-dimensional image shown in two dimensions. It's meant to be folded upwards to make a 3D room with eight walls, like a hoogan. You are seated in the center facing east, with west is behind you. Your internal Akbal extends above and below you, connecting your 7 chakras, as it flows through your 3D mind.

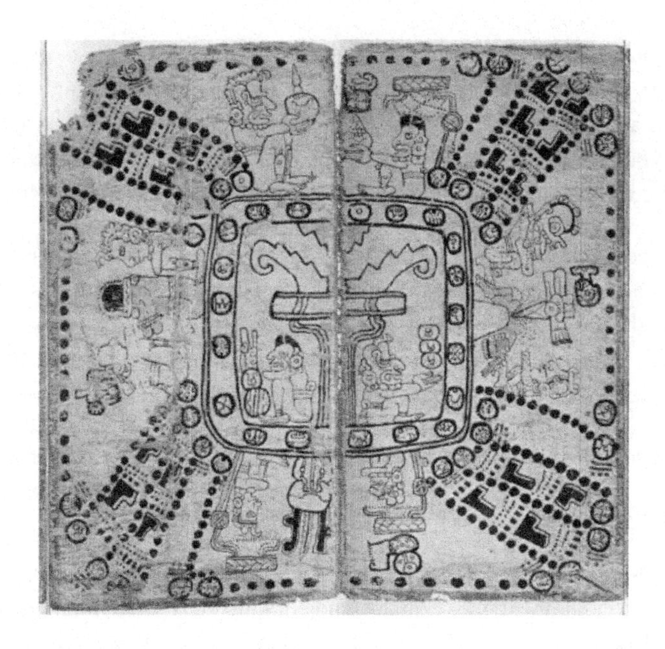

Once folded up into 3D, the walls and corners face each other. East faces west, north faces south, northwest faces southeast and northeast faces southwest. it is a simple matter to connect the dots (no pun intended). The Seed trecena passes along the top of the back wall of the hoogan. It also passes the top of the back wall of your mind. Wrapping the Tzolk'in in a 3D model like this, you see the connection between the Tzolk'in and the human mind. This is the Tzolk'in Clock. It explains our social interrelations and ourselves.

The flame (or Akbal) in the center is your mechanism for choice. You decide to accept/reject/ignore thoughts and that choice determines your next thought. The west face (behind you) is our collective consciousness. The right side depicts you as enslaved in your mind/body and the left side is transformed, like birth, sleeping, or death. The process of offering and receiving are shown on the east and west faces.

8-Monkey (A Woman's Perspective)

Let's say you are at home raising children and you depend on their father, your husband, to take care of material things. You and he share the same Akbal (heart) of the Tzolk'in Clock. Use the timing of this Clock by having him actively do things necessary to create your family's fruition. You planted your seeds on the east face. The seeds travelled through your sleep consciousness on the north face. They now travel through our collective consciousness on the west face. After 8-Monkey, there is interaction between your physical self and the Tzolk'in Clock on the south face. It's time to actively complete the process. Yet, you are not able to do more than what you are doing. So, it's up to your man to complete the process. Give him the wisdom to complete the seeds-to-fruition process after 8-Monkey.

The seed trecena is deeply connected to the web. Meditation this trecena effects all life consciousness. Based on the Hopi prophecy, this is the time to reunify the four directions. The Hopi says that about 500 years ago the re-unification of our four directions should have happened, and they say now is another time for it to happen.

"We need to be united as a people of the Human race." — *Stormy Deer*

Hoogans, the Tzolk'in Clock and the Human Mind

These three pictures on the next page show the outside of a hoogan, a flatted 3D representation of the Tzolk'in and looking into your mind from your heart chakra.

The human mind (bottom picture) shows your experience as the gold key in the center. Thoughts enter your mind from the east and you use the morals from the collective consciousness to accept, reject or ignore the thought. That choice determines the next thought to enter your mind. The right side of your mind mirrors the left side of your brain. The left side of your brain has logic, speech, writing, cognitive senses and math capabilities. The left side of your mind mirrors the right side of your brain. The right brain has imagination and creativity, which connects your consciousness to the collective create consciousness while you sleep.

The seed trecena connects us to our collective consciousness which gives us understanding of right vs. wrong. Morals are shown (bottom picture) as a map in the back of your mind. Your choice, or, choosing mechanism, is shown in the center. To the right are your cognitive abilities and to the left is your imagination.

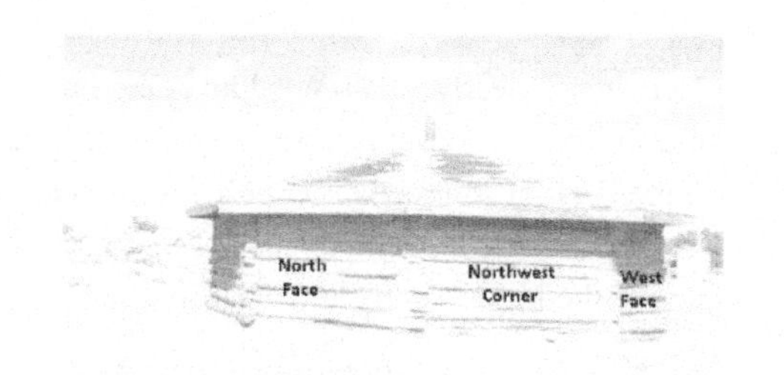
North
Face
Northwest
Corner
West
Face

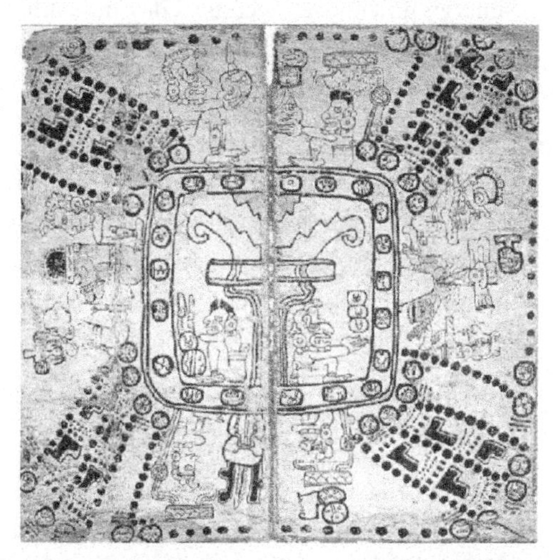

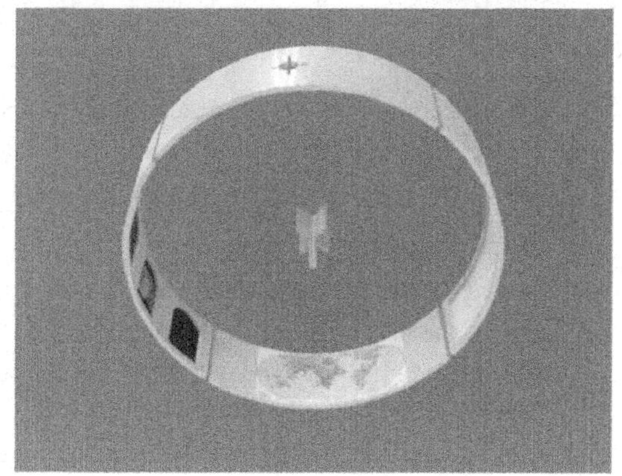

1-Seed	Between 1-Seed and 13-Wisdom is the time we update our collective consciousness. It is also at time we update ourselves. This trecena is excellent for meditation. Use the ebb and flow of the trecena. This trecena is also about shedding regrets and cleansing your heart.
2-Serpent	Yesterday's energy hit terminal velocity, like a sports car in first gear, and will coast through today, as the Serpent energy unwinds to become a day of death, ancestry and birth. There are energetic tides of nighttime energy today. Go with the flow.
3-Transformer	People born today will have the 11-Jaguar elder outlook. They keep their home as a nature sanctuary and retreat from the rest of the world. A place where others can rest and relax and feel surrounded by the tranquil peace of nature (the hills, the trees, the birds, the deer, the wild rabbits, squirrels, raccoons, possums).
4-Deer	Today is for stretching morals and shaking them clean to pull the worthless regrets off your soul.
5-Star	Today is the energy of dreamers, performers, and artists. It's a day to shine with our cleansed soul and rejoice in life. It is a pure and inspiring energy to be shared by others.
6-Water	Let the energy of 6-Water cleanse your consciousness. Connect with earth's consciousness. Let today's energy carry you rather than swim against it.
7-Dog	Today is the last day on the right side of the brain (left side of the mind). Tomorrow is the first day on the left side of the brain (right side of the mind). Many consider tomorrow to be the first day on the Tzolk'in round. It's the day to initiate new shamans. It's like we've spent the past 130 days dreaming and now we will spend the next 130 days doing something about it, to make our dreams into reality.

8-Monkey	Today is about listening to others and sharing appreciation to others. It is the love to listen to others and see them fully express themselves. This is an especially touching gift to know each other. You are a gift to everyone around you. Peace, love, and wisdom! Health, wealth and happiness this new year to you and yours!
9-Road	Today is a day of destiny. It's like the sun is lighting your future path as you are reminded of where you have been each of your previous 9-Road days, like looking through an old photo album. You also get glimpses of your future self.
10-Reed	Today is a close connection to our maker. You sense God's (father sky's) presence and feel the un-realness to this reality—a lifting of the veil, so to speak. Meditate on your faithfulness, fidelity, loyalty, and devotion. You are important in this relationship and can break trust and lose respect in the web.
11-Jaguar	Jaguar is your stairway to heaven. This is the connection with mother earth using big pads of a jaguar's foot. Their large paws touch sacred earth as you move through the reeds of yesterday and begin to jump to the eagle tomorrow.
12-Eagle	Today we soar into the night energy on the west side, and this trecena is all about personal change. It's a day to see the big picture of who you are and why we are here.
13-Wisdom	Today is the energy emerging from deep depth of 12-Eagle to the highest height of 13-Wisdom. Pay attention to your dreams. Enjoy this natural "Sunday" of the trecena.

EARTH (EARTHQUAKE)

Our new collective consciousness is born from 1-Earth to 13-Water. The peak of this trecena is 7-House, the noblest day with a strong sense of community. 13-Water is the day our updated collective consciousness emerges. Just as a spider makes a new web each day, our collective consciousness makes a new web for the next Tzolk'in round inside of the Tzolk'in Clock.

The center of both the Maya and Aztec 260 day rounds shows a similar message in two different forms. In the Maya version, there are three symbols on the lower left at the Shaman's feet. The bottom symbol is the union of your sleep and awake self. The middle symbol is your present moment. The top symbol is the serpent energy of life. It is this union, between awake and asleep (or, left brain and right brain) that creates life and consciousness for us.

The "rain-god" Cha'ak is on the right, tossing three seeds in the air. This represents our bound selves making choices and, thus, creating the serpent energy of life. It is our union with our sleep consciousness, or Nawal, and our wake consciousness that gives life.

The Aztec version shows a man holding the bondage (three arrows) in his right hand and the Serpent energy of life in his left hand, a device to throw the arrows. You are the human in the center.

It also shows how the chakra energies connect to different faces and corners of the Tzolk'in Clock. Four of those connects are clearly shown connecting to each of the four corners. The first chakra is connected to the west face. The seventh chakra is connected to east face. The fourth chakra connects the north and south face, the left brain and right brain, and your asleep and awake self.

Do you ever look back at past activities and wonder why it is less important now? Each time our web is updated (and celebrated on 8-Monkey) our collective sense of right and wrong changes. This slightly changes our morals each Tzolk'in round, which in turn, affects all of us. The Tzolk'in Clock explains our social and personal connections with time.

The previous page shows you as a Shaman and Cha'ak our "rain god" known for his crusty eyes, lighting (serpent energy) and holding bundles. Perhaps this God is your personal Nawal, or sleep self. Do we have individual sleep selves or are all connected to Cha'ak? Are we connected to one of the four directions? After you die, does your Nawal continue as an individual or part of a collective? Think of a leaf leaving a tree. The leaf returns all of its energy to the tree before falling off brown and lifeless.

From the east to center to west, your Nawal gets younger as you get older. This is showing how our lives are like leaves of a tree and the tree is our Nawal, or "rain god" Cha'ak. And, just as a leaf gives its life energy back to the tree before falling, we give life energy back to Cha'ak when we die. It's almost as if our lives are a recharging station for our Nawal. Perhaps the Maya knew more about that than we currently know. I can only imagine ball games at night with the Milky Way in the sky. There are many mysteries, and death is one of them. Perhaps the Tzolk'in sheds some light about where we are and why life is meaningful beyond death. At the age of 52, you gain perspective on this physical realm. It's from this time forward that your Nawal really gains its youth. The longer you live, the more beneficial it is to your Nawal.

Peace on Earth

During the previous Seed trecena, the crossing from our right (sleep) side to our left (enslaved) side has resonated with our spirits and emotions. It's interesting that the Tzolk'in was created around the time Jesus died. It's said his last words were not in any known language but easily recognized by the Maya and that it translates to, "Now I immerse myself in the pre-dawn of your presence." Perhaps the new *baktun* we all heard about in 2011/2012 was the dawn of our awakening.

What Would an Awakened World be Like?

Simply put, everyone would behave ethically so we could all always trust each other. As the awakening happens, those with defective minds can be healed. Ultimately, there would be no laws, no jails, no police, no borders, no lawyers, no taxes, no government and no wars. You wouldn't have locks on your doors, nor fear any intruders. Collectively, the weakest person would get the most attention, so everyone has a good and balanced life. We wouldn't need money, as our spiritual side would allow us to use our internal God-like powers more effectively. Things like the great pyramids of Egypt, and better, could be done with modern technology. This is all possible with one simple change in the human mind, and that is, we all behave ethically, without guilt and shame, using clean morals. Our web collectively defines right and wrong.

Yet, today, we mostly think about legal documents to complete. For instance, to enroll your kids in school they need shots, past grades, birth certificates, medical forms, etc. All of these legal documents have human names in capital letters. Of course you have to show your driver's license and credit card (both are backed by your legal name) to complete the legal documents. The time it takes for each child's parents to complete of those forms, get the shots, and pay the bills is not a healthy operating system, and is just one example.

Collectively, our web can be better than this. We can make a better web. This is the re-unification of the four directions.

1-Earthquake	Watch your thoughts, weed out negativity, and planting loving thoughts in your mind. Today is another first day of a new trecena to plant seeds, groom existing plants and weed a few out. Implement something new in your life today and see how effective it becomes over the next 13 days.
2-Flint	The energy of life is vibrant as we delve into the duality of our spirit to see what we like and what we don't like. There is plenty to remove to make room for more goodness. Be careful having an internal sharp knife swinging around inside of you. Stay focused. Make a mess.
3-Storm	Hold your family as water showers upon you, like a waterfall or an ocean's wave. It's a refreshing storm that cleanses yesterday's clippings. Cherish our gift of life. Rejoice in new abundance.
4-Light	Relax and enjoy today's energy. It is the most fragrant of all days.
5-Crocodile	Today's energy feels like 3-Storm, but personal. It's a day to say, "I'm sorry." It's also a day of collective consciousness awakening with positive community outlooks. Spread your smile.
6-Wind	The energy of wind enters your Akbal today. This is sacred energy from the breath of God. It's a source of life. Open your windows and let the breeze inside. Imagine an Akbal (spiritual flame) burning in your home. Today is the day to give blessings to the fire as the 6-Wind feeds it. When a fire burns, it creates new water. The consciousness of the water is the moment it was born. Bless the spiritual flame in your house for it creates new life with new water.
7-House	Center yourself in your Akbal today. Imagine how you want it with all the ability of our creator to provide it for you. Improve your current home surroundings today.

8-Seed	If there was a grand parent's day, it should be today. Spend time with your extended family.
9-Serpent	Feel the connection with your Nawal today and carefully watch your thoughts. Learn how to control them. Let your thoughts flow without accepting or rejecting them.
10-Transformer	This is a karma day. The best thing to do is appreciate your personal luxuries while not letting bad karma upset your balance. If you can make it through today, the next three days will be easy.
11-Deer	After yesterdays transformation, today is a day of stability, to get a new grip for the next twenty days. It's also a day of patience. Respect nature and her rules.
12-Star	There is a major shift in energy as our new web of life is set into place for this Tzolk'in round.
13-Water	Today is an offering day, a good day to pay bills and have extra money. "The secret to being rich is to spend less than you make; then you always have money." It's also a 13 day, the end of a trecena. It's a natural "Sunday" to relax and enjoy the fruit of your thoughts from the past 12 days. It's also a day to prepare new seeds for the start of the Dog Trecena. Play your favorite music to go with this magical energy.

DOG

The Dog trecena celebrates what makes us human and is a time to appreciate the special place of being human in this realm. Music is a good example of something appreciated by humans. It's impossible to imagine life without it. Don McLean wrote a song about it called *Bye, Bye Miss American Pie.*

We have just completed the west face (Monkey, Seed and Earth trecenas) of the Tzolk'in Clock. Now, we begin the Dog and House trecenas of the southwest corner. Shown between these two trecenas is the tail of your serpent energy, being bound and emerging as a flower with seeds. A vulture, flying over 1-House, picks up your seed to carry it to your fruition. The serpent energy enters three "trecenas of enslavement," (the south face) to produce your flower. These are the seeds of your future self on their way to becoming your fruition. The bird carries the seeds of your future self to produce your fruition on the south face and the southeast corner of the Tzolk'in Clock, ending with 13-Light (Ahau).

This southwest corner also connects with your second chakra (shown as red blood/energy).

Your seeds, planted on the Crocodile trecena, must interact with the physical realm in order to come to fruition. This interaction is shown with Serpent energy passing inside of three containers, which represent the three trecenas of the south face. It's during the southwest corner that our seeds flower, then the bird transfers our seeds, and during the southeast corner they come to fruition. The seeds of your future self were presented, examined and contemplated by our collective consciousness on the west face of the Tzolk'in Clock. You can feel your future self being examined inside of a hoogan. Your seeds are now ready to enter your physical reality to emerge as fruit on the south face of the Tzolk'in Clock.

The day of 1-Dog is a gathering day for all people born on the first inflection of the 20 different Nawal day signs. Each of the 20 Nawal day signs has a unique gift for humanity. Collectively, the 20 Nawal day signs embody all that being human has to offer. This gathering of the Nawal day signs will have a resonance for each of the thirteen inflections this trecena. For example, if you were born on the fifth inflection, you will have an extra resonance with the fifth day of this trecena. This ripples all the way through the trecena until 13-Wind, when, collectively, this energy is released into our consciousness.

The Dog Trecena Tunes Our Web of Collective Consciousness

Our web of collective consciousness was set in place on the last trecena (Earth to Water). This web connects to the first inflection of all 20 trecenas within the Tzolk'in Clock. On 1-Dog, all people born on the first inflection gather to set the fundamental vibration of our collective web of consciousness. On the second day, all humans born on the second inflection carry this energy and add their vibrations to the web. And, so on through this trecena, until 13-Wind. That is the day, we let go of the web for the next Tzolk'in round. Imagine the Tzolk'in folded up into 3D. The foundation of the web of consciousness, inside of the Tzolk'in Clock, connects at each 1 day of all 20 trecenas. The dog energy ripples like a wave, 1 through 13. Each day of this trecena is another ripple in the wave. You will feel it when it's your turn. It depends on your birth inflection (1, 2, 3…etc.).

The Tzolk'in Clock is a doorway out of the box you have been given. It's a harmonious way to tell time. It can unlock your full potential as a human. Collectively, it can re-unite the four directions. There is a revolution happening within the white northern direction and fire element. A new consciousness is emerging for this *baktun*. The winner will be wholesome and true. There are many of us who know the problem, the solution and the outcome of this awakening that began recently and will continue for thousands of years. Peace on Earth

The west face of the Tzolk'in as depicted on the Aztec Tzolk'in is very similar to images found between the Caspian and Black Seas.

The west face is located at the receiving end of thoughts, where morals (the collective consciousness of right and wrong) is located. As the collective consciousness changes, so do our morals. There is one source of thought (GOD or YOU) and one source of morals (all of us). Do you choose thoughts as they are sent to you? Or, do you create thoughts? Once you have a thought, realize that you accept, reject or ignore it. Depending on that choice, determine the next thought. We use morals to decide right from wrong. If we chose to do wrong, a black, sticky guilt enters our mind. This is difficult to get out of your mind once it's created. As more and more guilt builds up, it is harder to see right from wrong. The highest state of mind, is to live in the moment (not worrying about the future, nor regretting the past) and make guilt-free choices.

1-Dog	This trecena starts with a bang, both creatively and physically. Share your passion. This is the beginning of the trecena that celebrates all humans. People born on the first inflection should gather.
2-Monkey	Weave your time like a diagram on a spider's web or a design on a loom. People born on the second inflection should gather.
3-Road	Chose your direction, time and place. Today is a day for new direction in life. It's a good day to set out on an adventure. People born on the third inflection should gather.
4-Reed	4 days are smooth sailing, stable days. Reed days are the connection between you and God. People born on the fourth inflection should gather.
5-Jaguar	Dr. Carl Calleman's Tzolk'in birthday! You learn about the day's energy by knowing people born on that day. You especially want to be around your friends on their Maya birthdays. People born on the fifth inflection should gather.
6-Eagle	Today is a mysterious day to confront your inner fears. People born on the sixth inflection should gather.
7-Wisdom	Today is a high place for thinking. People born on the seventh inflection should gather.
8-Earth	This is the day the Eagle/Wisdom energy penetrates the earth to collect flint for tomorrow. People born on the eighth inflection should gather.
9-Flint	Today is a fertile day to cut things out of your life that you don't like. People born on the ninth inflection should gather.
10-Storm	Let the wind blow away all of your clippings from yesterday. It's a day to clear your soul, spirit and mind. People born on the tenth inflection should gather.
11-Light	Walk on sunshine. Spend time outside on a Dog trecena. It's a good day for the park. People born on the eleventh inflection should gather.

12-Crocodile	This is a night time emergence in calm, placid waters. The water is deep. How deep can you go before you become afraid of drowning and come up for air? Use the strength of a crocodile to immerse yourself deep into your spirit. Calmly rise to the surface and view your surroundings. People born on the twelfth inflection should gather.
13-Wind	It's interesting that the upside down T shape is found in ancient buildings from Peru to the Navajo nation. This symbol is on windows and doors all over the Americas. Imagine if another dimension was living here with us, and they can be here with us, like we see fish in a large aquarium. We don't even know their presence. It's the breath from this dimension—the place we go when we sleep—that is in our house. We are all in our own bodies and physical surroundings, breathing. The T is also the Maya sign for Wind, which is always the day before House. People born on the thirteenth inflection should gather.

ON CONSCIOUSNESS

Ian Lungold's videos teach us about the living spirit of time. He clearly shows us how a calendar is the center of our collective consciousness. At the beginning of his presentations, he asks, "What is consciousness?" His answer is, "being aware that you are aware." It is that awareness that is our consciousness. Watching his videos is a must to understand the impact of this book.

I believe there are levels of consciousness which I call fractal levels. For illustration, let us say a snail has a fractal level of 1, a dog has a fractal level of 5 and a human has a fractal level of 10. Humans have the full capabilities of consciousness, whereas a dog cannot speak, and a snail is not aware of our presence. Another metaphor is to say a tree's trunk is fractal level of 1, branches are level 5 and the whole tree is level 10. It is our level 10 consciousness that allows us to reason and use speech and writing. I often joke that some humans have a level 9.9 and other a level 10.1, when referring to levels of intelligence. When a person dies, that unique collection of spirits will never occupy the same consciousness again.

I have reasoned that our consciousness is made up of individual "spirits" that collectively occupy our mind when we are awake. These "spirits" leave our mind when we fall asleep. The instant you wake up, they collectively enter your mind. When you die, the spirits leave your mind forever and go back into the infinite pool of spirits. Sometime after conception and before birth, a new group of individual spirits is gathered and put into the newborn to be together for the rest of its life. Perhaps this is when "morning sickness" occurs. The quantity of spirits required for life may vary. For instance, a mosquito may only have one spirit, but a bird may have twenty. Perhaps humans have a billion spirits? The individual spirits recycle, and you are a unique combination that will never be together again. Some of your spirits may have occupied the mind of someone famous.

The south face of the Madrid codex Tzolk'in illustrates this collection of spirits. It shows that operation of your mind is on the south face and the portal from awake to asleep and back is on the north face. The north face illustrates your consciousness leaving your body when you sleep, and, ultimately, when you die.

The book *Three Magic Words* presents the argument, "Do we create thoughts or are thoughts sent to us?" US Anderson's answer is that thoughts are sent to us. The book, *A Stroke of Insigh*t, explains how the left and right sides of your brain operate. Combine these two ideas into the Tzolk'in Clock and you see that thoughts are projected into your mind from the east face (the door of a hogan) while you sit inside and make choices to accept, reject or ignore those thoughts. Behind you is the collective consciousness off all life helping you make these choices. The west face of the Tzolk'in Clock is the location of your morals and knowing right from wrong. You make the right choices that feel good. Bad choices make you feel guilt, which makes it dirty in the area behind you, so you must keep it clean. The best way to keep your mind clean is not to make choices that make you feel guilty. Guilt is the rudder through your steam of thoughts and this rudder is directly connected to your morals. It feels good to keep your hoogan and mind clean. The Tzolk'in Clock lets you know the right time in this regard. For instance, the Flint trecena is a good time to deeply clean your hoogan mind, just before the west face of the Tzolk'in Clock begins.

Here is a detailed explanation of the Tzolk'in Clock from your mind's perspective. Touch just above your right eyebrow, using your left hand. Go straight up to the top of your forehead. That is the Crocodile trecena. Now go across your forehead. That is the Jaguar trecena. Go down to your left eyebrow. That is the Deer trecena. All three of those trecenas are the east wall of the Tzolk'in Clock. Now go up, over and down your left temple. Those are the Light (going up) and Reed (going down) trecenas. This pattern continues around your head. Go up and over and down your left ear. Those are the Transformer, Storm and Road trecenas of the north face / left side of your mind / right side of your brain. There is no ego on this side of the Tzolk'in Clock. Each night, when we fall asleep, our consciousness leaves the prison of our physical selves. It is during the north face of the Tzolk'in Clock that our spiritual selves work on the seeds we planted on the east face of the Tzolk'in Clock. The north face of the Tzolk'in Clock is when and where your individual spirits that make up your consciousness go their separate ways. They scatter your intentions into the collective consciousness like seeds in the wind. Each morning, when you wake up, they all return, the veil is closed, and your consciousness is contained. Your awake self is back in control. The Tzolk'in Clock is all about using the collective consciousness to create your physical reality. The north face of the Tzolk'in Clock is the time to weave your dreams into reality. With all the power of our creator, imagine your reality as you want it to be. This is the time to build on the seeds that you planted on the east face of the Tzolk'in Clock. Use your intuition to know what really can become reality and focus your spiritual intentions on those fertile plants. The Rainstorm trecena of the north face is the deepest spiritual trecena. It is equivalent to traveling through the right brain of consciousness. Dr. Jill Taylor explains the right brain of consciousness in her book, *A Stroke of Insight.* She describes the right brain (north face of the Tzolk'in Clock) as euphoria of the intuitive and a sense of complete well-being and peace. Comparing the Tzolk'in Clock to a human brain, the Rainstorm trecena is deep in the right brain. This trecena is a time for meditation. Put pure ingredients into your body. It is a good time for fasting, purification and staying away from poisonous items like alcohol.

Put your finger on the left back side of your head and go up. This is the Monkey trecena. Go across and down the right back side of your head. Those are the Seed and Earth trecenas, completing the west face of the Tzolk'in Clock. Guilt can build up on the west face and have a spiraling effect to make choosing right from wrong harder to see.

In three dimensions, your mind has corners and walls. Your east wall faces the west wall, and your north wall faces the south wall. Your northeast corner faces the southwest corner, and your northwest corner faces the southeast corner. Using this analogy, you can envision the seed trecena passing along the top of the back (west) wall of your mind, the hoogan, and the Tzolk'in Clock. Wrapping the Tzolk'in in a 3D model like this, you see the connection between the Tzolk'in and the human mind. The Tzolk'in Clock explains our social interrelations and ourselves. Your consciousness is the gold key located in the center of your mind. Thoughts enter your mind from the east and you use the morals from the collective consciousness to accept, reject or ignore the thought. That choice determines the next thought to enter your mind.

The mind and brain are mirror images, just like the left side of your brain controls the right side of your body and vice versa. The left side of your mind (north face of the Tzolk'in Clock) connects with the right side of your brain. The right brain has imagination, creativity and connects your consciousness to the collective consciousness while you sleep. The north face is the veil between your awake self and your asleep self, or your conscious enslaved self and your freed unconscious self. The left side of your brain has logic, speech, writing, cognitive senses, and math capabilities. The right side of your mind (south face) connects the left side of your brain. The south face of the Tzolk'in Clock shows three trecenas going around an enslaved man. You can see his arms and legs bound and his head encapsulated. South face trecenas with our left brain which involve the use of our intelligence (speaking, counting, logic, music, and dance) and our connections with the physical world using our senses (touch, taste, sound, sight, and smell).

The opposite north face of the Tzolk'in Clock has three trecenas go around a man set free from his body. This joining and separation begins at birth, every time you sleep, and ends at death. The north face is the veil between your awake self and your asleep self, or your conscious enslaved self and your freed unconscious self. The north face of the Tzolk'in Clock is like the right brain of a human. The Maya had nunneries that taught about our physical spirit and our sleep spirit (Nawal). The south face of the Tzolk'in Clock shows a human enslaved. The north face of the Tzolk'in Clock shows a human being freed from his consciousness. The joining and separation begin at birth, every time you sleep, and ends at death.

The south and north faces relate to the left and right brain. The east and west faces are about your thoughts and choices. The east face is where thoughts enter your mind. Shown in the center of the Tzolk'in Clock are three choices: accept, reject, or ignore. The west face is where the collective consciousness gives us guidance for our choices. Thoughts become ideas that become reality. Inventions, art, and music get their inspiration from human thought.

The west face shows your awake self offering a seed (goal/intention) to your sleep self who is connected to our collective consciousness. This is the seed you conceived on the east face. Your seeds will be judged by our collective consciousness along the west face. Also, our collective consciousness will be updated as we travel along the west face. The west face is about our collective morals and right versus wrong. This is the time when our seeds get judged and appreciated. On the west side, we immerse ourselves into the collective consciousness. Our morals are based on our collective consciousness, knowing right from wrong, based on what we collectively believe. You might say the east side is the pitcher of thoughts and the west side is the catcher, and we steer the ball along the way.

Sometimes, people have trouble making decisions, and people on the west (the catchers) are good at helping us make decisions by giving advice and leadership. Imagine you are in a hoogan and the west face is on the wall behind you, as you face east. When thoughts enter your mind in front, you chose to accept, reject, or ignore based on the morals on the back, west face.

Imagine the west face of the hoogan as the collective consciousness connected to your mind as you make choices, deciding what is right and what is wrong. You sit in the center of your hoogan as thoughts stream in through the front door on the east face. If you choose to do something that makes you feel guilty, it is based on the morals of our collective consciousness on the west face. The space between you in the center and the west face of the hoogan should be the cleanest. This is your personal connection with life. The west face of the Tzolk'in Clock is the status of all living consciousness. Each time we pass through the west face, our collective consciousness is updated. Our understanding of right and wrong is different since our great great grandparents, and it will be different for our great, great grandchildren.

The flame (or, Akbal) in the center is your mechanism for choosing to accept/reject/ignore thoughts and that choice determines your next thought. The west face, behind you, is our collective consciousness. The south face is enslaved in our mind/body and the north face is transformed, like birth, sleeping, or death. The process of offering and receiving are shown on the east and west sides. Every 260 days the cycle repeats. This is how the 3D version of the Tzolk'in Clock frames your mind.

I have spent years trying to figure out what the artist meant when he drew the 260-day Tzolk'in round in Madrid Codex, written well before the arrival of European influences. Many books have been written about the Olmec, Maya and Aztec cultures following the same 260-day cycle. As far as I can tell, all living Maya agree on a 260-day cycle (Tzolk'in, Choil-qu, and Tonamalli). This validates that each day is truly as we think it is and it has not changed since its inception thousands of years ago.

I have found only a few books that go into the details of the Tzolk'in as depicted in the Madrid Codex. *The Cosmos of the Yucatec Maya: Cycles and Steps from the Madrid Codex* by Merideth Paxton, *2000 Years of Maya Literature* by Dennis Tedlock, and *Maya Cosmos* by David Freidel, Linda Schele and Joy Parker.

INSPIRATION

My hesitation and inspiration to publish this work is that I have not lived in Guatemala where the Tzolk'in is practiced today. Yet, the Tzolk'in as depicted in the Madrid codex has not appeared in many books and the Maya that I have met have not heard of this depiction. Could many of the messages that it contains have been forgotten? My hope is that this work will be well received, and a second publication can be made, after visiting and collaborating with the living Maya. One advantage I have is that my ideas have not been influenced by contemporary beliefs and I am taking this from the approach of learning what was written over 500 years ago.

If you have found your way to reading this book, then you likely know about the Tzolk'in. After reading all the books available on the topic, there are only a few that specifically address the Tzolk'in and this book is the only one, that I know of, written about the spiritual aspect of it.

Chronologically, as I discovered each meaning in this book, my ideas became more complex as each idea built upon the previous. How does your mind work? How does your mind manifest your reality? Why do you sleep and how does sleep connect to your consciousness?

Three Magic Words by US Anderson was given to me by my grandmother when I was a teenager. It presents the idea of where thoughts originate and suggests a 30-day mental diet of watching your thoughts. At the end of each chapter, there is a pleasant meditation.

That book led me to understand how our mind works. Over the years I visualized my mind and how I see thoughts and either accept, reject, or ignore them. I also learned to use guilt as a rudder for my decisions. I learned to make choices that do not add guilt in my mind. Guilt is like a black goo that accumulates and makes it harder to know right from wrong.

In the visualization of my mind, guilt builds up on the "window" of morals located at the receiving end of thoughts, and effects the choices we make.

The story behind the centuries-long decipherment of ancient Maya hieroglyphs aired April 8, 2008 on PBS, called *Cracking the Maya Code.* I was inspired by the Maya use of a combination of vowels and pictures to make words. All other languages on earth are either phonetic *or* pictures, never both.

Further research led me to a video, *Secrets of the Mayan Calendar Unveiled* presented by Ian Xel Lungold on September 6, 2003 at Okanagan University College in Vernon, Canada. This video (https://youtu.be/O9THJgpYbVY) explains how important a calendar is to everyone and how our collective consciousness has evolved. He clearly demonstrates how the Tzolk'in relates to our collective consciousness and time. His work is based on Carl Johan Calleman's book, *Solving the Greatest Mystery of Our Time: The Mayan Calendar.* Dr. Calleman scientifically and factually demonstrates how time connects all of us.

While learning about the Tzolk'in and our collective consciousness, I was working on my own ideas of consciousness. Few people I have met even know why we sleep. I ask and the typical response is that our body needs rest. When pressed for which part of our body, most people say our mind. When pressed further for which part of our mind, a few people respond correctly with: our consciousness. Yes, our consciousness does leave our body when we sleep as explained in the work of Jill Taylor's, *A Stroke of Insight.* She is a PhD neurologist who experienced a stroke and clearly demonstrates how our left and right brain are connected to our spiritual selves. This relationship is shown in the Madrid codex version of the Tzolk'in. It shows your consciousness enslaved in your mind on one side and it shows your consciousness released from your body on the other side. To know the Tzolk'in, you must be open to ancient ways. You must know how your conscious works. You must be open to the idea of a collective consciousness.

Most of my content comes from the Tzolk'in as depicted in the Fejervary and Madrid codices. These are the only two sources. I am sure there would be more, but Diego de Landa gathered the books of the Maya in 1562 and burnt them. This is a common practice when you want to remove the indigenous culture and replace it with your own. It was not until 1952 that Yuri Knorosov cracked the "hieroglyphic" code. Now we can at least read what is written in the few remaining books. Recently, in 2018, a new technology known as Lidar revealed millions more Maya ruins than previously thought, and I am hoping new codices will be discovered—especially one with another depiction of the Tzolk'in.

Who created the Tzolk'in? It has been written in many sources that the Olmec created Tzolk'in and the Maya received it from Olmecs. Then the Aztecs either received it from Olmecs or the Maya. One ambitious author even claimed the last words spoken by Jesus was in the Maya language. His last words were not in any known language but easily recognized by the Maya, translated to, "Now I immerse myself in the pre-dawn of your presence." Perhaps the new *baktun* that we all heard about on both October 28, 2011 (13-Ahau) and December 21, 2012 (4-Ahau) is the dawn of our awakening. The Tzolk'in did come in existence at the time of many other new religions: Christianity, Islam, and Buddhism. It's unknown exactly who, when and how the Tzolk'in was manifested.

Another Mesoamerican calendar is the Ha'ab, which is based on the seasonal cycle of the sun. Every Ha'ab year, the day is shifted from sunrise to noon, or noon to sunset, or sunset to midnight, or midnight to sunrise. This way the Ha'ab is perfectly in-sync with the season cycle without the need for a leap year. The equivalent European seasonal cycle, the Gregorian calendar, is off by a few seconds each year.

The Madrid codex version of the Tzolk'in was written before the European interference. The origin of the Madrid codex is unknown. Exactly how the Maya used it before being conquered are unknown. The European belief system has since created a mixture of Christian and Maya beliefs. This book attempts to view the Tzolk'in as it would have been before the arrival of Europeans. To the Maya, the earth was flat with an underworld, the sky, and the earth. The Tzolk'in was their religion and today, it remains a sacred, personal calendar.

The purpose of this book is to introduce my findings before returning to Guatemala, Mexico and Belize. I still have much to learn about the Tzolk'in. This is my first attempt to explain what it means as I see it today. In Texas, few, if any, people understand how the Tzolk'in works with our collective consciousness. People living on the Gregorian calendar aren't aware of living on spiritual time. Living on Tzolk'in time connects you with our creator and this power is offered to you so that you may manifest your reality. All people manifest their reality, but the Tzolk'in keeps the time.

FINAL THOUGHTS

In September 2011, I travelled to Centre Lothlorien in France to a Peace Festival for my first experience with Maya Guatemala Grandmothers Elisabeth Aurojo and Nana Vilma and Maya Colombians Paco and Nasly Quiroga. The schedule said they would do their morning ceremony at 9AM. Events were scheduled by the hour, but they were nowhere to be found. As nearly 100 of us waited in a large circle, they arrived from the nearby river. The translator said that their concept of time is different than ours. It sent a ripple through the obligatory schedule that has resonated with me since. The Gregorian (Ha'ab equivalent) will be useful for manifesting your reality, especially as we flow through the water trecena.

My mission, after visiting Tikal in 2016, compelled me to look up everyone's Mayan birthdays. It amazed me how many people are interested to know this. Several times while doing this, someone would be especially interested to know about it. And, when I focused on this person, it turned out to be their Maya birthday. How else would they have known? I have also looked up people that have the same birthday as me. It is a special day when you get to meet someone born on your Mayan birthday. It's like seeing yourself in a spiritual mirror. I have looked up people that are directly opposite of me on the Tzolk'in Clock. There is a special relationship (that I call a soulmate) when you meet someone directly opposite.

You begin to see patterns as you meet people and learn their Mayan birthdays. I've found people born on the west side (moral side) to be good at managing other people. People on the south side (left brain) are good at math, language, and logic. People born on the east (where thoughts originate) tend to help others get along with each other. People on the north side (right brain) are good at artistic expression.

It is the positively strong spiritual connections I experienced during this research that compelled me to write the twenty articles and this book. It's my hope that spiritual time will resonate with you, especially if you tired of living on materialistic time.

Something did not seem right when I visited both Tonina and Palenque. The amount of work needed to create these cities seemed to be too much for humans. Tonina was once thought to be just another mountain until it was uncovered in 2010. Consider that a 20 lb. stone is roughly 3" x 1' x 1'. Each stone needs to be cut, transported, and placed into the proper position. Tonina is roughly 10 million ft^3 of stone. (1500'x800'x250' high / 3). That is 50 million stones. Let us say a human can cut, transport and place 10 stones a day and there are 5000 people working together. It would take 10,000 days or 28 years to complete. Most of the work is just laying the foundation to get 40 feet into the air.

I recently asked Xikinch'o, a stone carver who lives in Xcaret, Mexico how the Maya could do this without metal tools. His response was, "to me as a carver, I can say, work in lime stone is possible with the use of harder stones like jade tools, obsidian tools, hammers of hard wood, and a lot of workers repeating cuts a thousand times."

Little was known about the Maya civilization in the late 1800s. However, many speculations have been normalized as the truth. There are so many people saying it was due to scarcity of food that the Maya civilization collapsed with little or any thought given to their ways of perception. Ball games can only vaguely be described, and few people mention anything other than it is like basketball. They do not mention which days it was played and any interaction with non-human entities, such as their spiritual guides. Activities such as sacrifice make little sense to us. Once inside the mindset of the Maya, you can see that your spirit self lives beyond your awake self and the human sacrifice is not as scary.

Dine' is the name that the Navajo use for themselves. Navajo is a European name given to them. Besides all the reasons mentioned for my belief in the Tzolk'in/hoogan connection, there is another reason. It involves seeing entities beyond our "normal" experiences. I want to share this experience and have permission from my Dine' shaman. Most people dismiss this experience because it is too far or out of their box to appreciate. I do not know how you will use this information, but if you visit the Dine', show them the respect that their ancient knowledge deserves.

During the 40 days that I lived with the Navajo, their hoogan gave me the idea to see the Tzolk'in drawn on the inside, just as I had envisioned it in my mind. Living in a hoogan is the most amazing way to experience time on earth. At night, the only way to see outside is through a square hole about two hands long and filled with the circular furnace stack. You can see a few stars if the sky is clear. You also feel very safe because there is only one door and it is not possible to open it when locked. The hoogan is direct replica of a Tzolk'in Clock mapped on the inner walls with an internal flame in the center, just as the hoogan has a furnace located in the center. Opening the front door before the sun rises and then watching the inside of the hoogan gradually fill with light gives you an amazing perception of time. What is even more interesting is how the Tzolk'in wraps around your consciousness and is a three dimensions model of your mind and connects to your chakras. My intention there was to bridge the gap between the Navajo and the Maya, including their abilities to see beyond the limitations of our five senses. During my visit, I explored the four corners of the Navajo nation looking for signs of the Tzolk'in in their petroglyphs, pictographs, and pottery. I also wanted to re-visit the portals in Canyon de Chelly from my previous visit. During that visit, I experienced portals to other dimensions and entities from other dimensions. These portals and entities are tied to the Anasazi people known as the "basket weavers." They are the ones who made the petroglyphs, pictographs, and pottery, and left sacred dwellings in the canyons of Arizona.

Few people outside of the Dine' know about the "Immortals" (or, inter-dimensional beings) that dwell in the canyons. Few people know about the entities that exist inside and roam above the canyons in the Navajo nation. You may be asking, "What is an entity?" I can only suggest that you consider that all matter has consciousness. The frequency of some consciousness, like stone, is so slow that our lives are like a mere flash in time to their consciousness. When I look closely at a pictograph, I see the color is not painted on the stone, but the grains inside the stone have changed color. Somehow a combination of the canyon, the dwellings and the pictographs increase the frequency of the stones consciousness so it can be experienced by humans.

I can only imagine how the first recording of the Tzolk'in came into existence. If it is divine, it may have been transferred from the same source of consciousness that I experienced in the Navajo nation. I often wonder if the same "Immortals" participated in the Maya ball games of the classical age, and if they interacted with the Olmecs, prior to the Maya.

In the canyons of the Navajo nation, each ancient Anasazi dwelling has a unique motif with different settings and different entities. You have to be in a peyote altered state of mind, touched by a Dine' shaman, and Pleiades should not be visible. At night, with the moon near full, you can see the entities that exist at each motif. I did not approach the sacred sites as it felt the same as being in a zoo. You would not enter the tiger cage. My first experience was The White House ruins in Canyon de Chelly. Its motif has portals connecting to another place. We viewed them from a distance. The entities and portals of White House have a powerful feel to them. There were many different types of entities and the portals had depth with side doors that could only be viewed if entered. The entities went in and out of the side doors. It appeared that a lagoon was on the other side of the portal, as viewed from a cave above the lagoon. I did have a desire to run through the portal. There was one large entity who stood in front of the White House and he appeared to be the protector of this motif or ancient ruin. This happened around midnight between 1-Dog and 2-Monkey on the evening of July 23, 2016, the beginning of the southwest corner of the Tzolk'in Clock.

Turning around, the motif behind us is that of a busy airport. Walking further down the canyon, the next motif was like the jungle with animal like entities. And the last one was a beautiful motif of a palace with two very tall, elegant entities. That was the end of the first night that I experienced entities from other dimensions. There are other locations with other motifs, the most impressive one beyond Spider Rock. I can only image the motifs beyond Spider Rock. I believe the entities at those motifs are called "The Immortals."

I returned to Spider Rock 209 days later between 2-Storm and 3-Ahau on the evening of February 17, 2017, the middle of the northwest corner of the Tzolk'in Clock. A few days later, on 8-Serpent, was my first experience with an entity on this visit. I was chopping wood with one of my Dine' guides. My dog was barking at a burnt and broken tree. The entity was wrapped around the trunk of the tree. As my dog continued to bark at it, it extended a transparent force that hit the dog. The dog yelped and ran away into the woods. My guide saw the entity, too. Later we found my dog in the back of the camper on the truck, scared and afraid.

I asked another Dine' guide about these entities and she told me one approached her in the canyon and stole her turquoise jewelry that she had just made. Another time, on 6-Wisdom, she and I were walking through the canyons of Sedona and she became very weak. We had walked past several dark entities that had drained her energy. Again, my dog ran away. He would not cross their path again and she needed rest to continue. The water that used to run through that part of the canyon was cut off about 100 years ago. These entities were not helpful to us. My other Dine' guide told me about seeing an entity growing up, too. However, none of this would prepare me for my own personal experience with an entity.

On the night between 7-Dog and 8-Monkey, I was alone in the hoogan, when a large "spider" immortal entity entered my space. Its eight legs connecting perfectly to the hoogan. It wanted to know what I was doing there. It seemed to know that I would not stop until I visited the heart of Spider Rock where "the royalty of the immortals" exists. The next day (8-Monkey), the canyon flooded. Several jeeps were swallowed by water (without injury), and treacherous trail hikes were prohibited. I was prevented from visiting as planned.

I think this picture is a painting of this sacred place. I noticed this in a video from my trip. Can you imagine interacting with an "Immortal" at this location at night?

Here is Carlos Cedillo's painting of our first encounter with the entities at White House.

Here is a photo of our group the night before we had our first encounter at White House.

I left the Navajo nation feeling like I had made several friends. I also began to see the Tzolk'in/hoogan relationship after this trip, which is a major portion of my discussions in the articles.

Made in the USA
Coppell, TX
19 January 2021